Students, Courses and Jobs

The Relationship Between Higher Education
and the Labour Market

Higher Education Policy Series 21

Students, Courses and Jobs

The Relationship Between Higher Education and the Labour Market

J.L. Brennan, E.S. Lyon, P.A. McGeevor
and K. Murray

Jessica Kingsley Publishers
London and Bristol, Pennsylvania

First published in the United Kingdom in 1993 by
Jessica Kingsley Publishers Ltd
116 Pentonville Road
London N1 9JB, England
 and
1900 Frost Road, Suite 101
Bristol, PA 19007, U S A

Copyright © 1993 J.L. Brennan, E.S. Lyon, P.A. McGeevor
and K. Murray

British Library Cataloguing in Publication Data
Students, Courses and Jobs: Relationship
Between Higher Education and the Labour
Market. - (Higher Education Policy
Series; No.21)
I Title II Series
378

ISBN 1-85302-538-0

Printed and Bound in Great Britain by
Bookcraft Ltd., Avon

Contents

	Preface	ix
1	The Project	1
2	The Research	12
3	Students and Courses into Employment	22
4	A Segmented Labour Market	48
5	The Changing Graduate Labour Market	57
6	Patterns of Graduate Destinations	74
7	The Stratified System of Higher Education	93
8	The Competent Graduate	109
9	Conclusions and Policy Implications	138
	Bibliography	145
	Index	147

List of Tables and Figures

Tab. 2.1   Helm project course types   13
Fig. 2.2a Polytechnics and colleges – how contact was made
           with the 1985 panel   15
Fig. 2.2b BTEC and university graduates in 1985 panel   16
Tab. 2.3   Response rate of the 1982 panel   17
Tab. 2.4   Response rate of the 1985 panel   18
Fig. 2.5   Contact points with the two graduate panels   20
Fig. 3.1   Students and courses in employment: an interactive
           model   26
Tab. 3.2   Proportions of students with 6 or more A-level points
           (1985 survey)   31
Tab. 3.3   Proportions of students with 9 or more A-level points
           (1985 survey)   32
Fig. 3.4   Job orientation type 'careerist'   35
Fig. 3.5   Job orientation type 'inner directed worker'   35
Fig. 3.6   Job orientation type 'altruistic orientation'   36
Fig. 3.7   Job orientation type 'leisure orientation'   36
Fig. 3.8   Reason for doing further study: personal interest   38
Fig. 3.9   Reason for doing further study: career prospects   38
Fig. 3.10 Job orientation by gender: male and female score   39
Fig. 3.11 Job orientation by age: mature and standard
           entrant score   40
Fig. 3.12 'Careerist orientation': parents' social class   40
Tab. 3.13 GCE & CSE examination passes by gender   42
Tab. 3.14 Subjects undertaken by graduate men and women   44
Tab. 3.15 Percentage of mature students at entry by course   45
Fig. 3.16 Proportions of fathers in senior professional and
           managerial jobs   46
Fig. 3.17 Proportions who attended grammar and fee paying
           schools   46
Fig. 5.1a Speed of entry into the labour market wave two,
           1982 panel   63
Fig. 5.1b Speed of entry into the labour market wave one,
           1985 panel   63
Fig. 5.2a Type of employing organisation wave two,
           1982 panel – women   64
Fig. 5.2b Type of employing organisation wave two,
           1982 panel – men   64
Fig. 5.2c Type of employing organisation wave one,
           1985 panel – women   65
Fig. 5.2d Type of employing organisation wave one,
           1985 panel – men   65

Fig. 5.3   Employment status two years after graduation by course
            and gender: wave two, 1982 panel   67
Fig. 5.4   Employment status two years after graduation by course
            and gender: wave one, 1985 panel   69
Tab. 6.1   Recruitment from courses by major types of job (wave one,
            1985)   76
Tab. 6.2   Percentage of recruits to major types of job recruited from
            five course types   81
Tab. 6.3   Type of educational institution attended by type of job   82
Tab. 6.4   1985 Graduates two years after graduation. Type of job
            by a-level point score and percentage of firsts or upper
            seconds   83
Tab. 6.5   Type of job by social background 1985 cohort   85
Tab. 6.6   Type of job by social background 1985 cohort   86
Tab. 6.7   Type of employer and salary   87
Tab. 6.8   Earnings of male and female full-time employees by
            type of work and employer (1985 cohort three and a
            half years after graduation)   88
Tab. 6.9   Employment status by stage of family formation and
            gender   89
Tab. 6.10   Mean salary of graduates in full-time employment by
            family formation   90
Tab. 6.11   Moving county or city as a result of work. Male and
            female graduates by stage of family formation   91
Tab. 6.12   Moving county or city as a result of partner's work:
            male and female graduates by stage of family
            formation   92
Fig. 7.1a   Unemployed graduates: 6 months after graduation   95
Fig. 7.1b   Full-time employment: 6 months after graduation   96
Fig. 7.1c   Training & further education: 6 months after graduation   97
Tab. 7.2   A-level points and O-level passes (1985 panel)   98
Tab. 7.3   Social background and secondary schooling
            1985 panel)   99
Tab. 7.4   Type of employment and category of employing
            organisation (1985 panel two years after graduation)   100
Tab. 7.5   Salary from principal occupation (1985 panel
            two years and three and a half years after graduation)   103
Tab. 7.6   Family background, degree classification and median
            salary after two years   104
Tab. 7.7   Aspects of job quality and career development   106
Fig. 8.1   O-level English by course: comparing the 1982 and 1985
            cohorts   112
Fig. 8.2   O-level Maths by course: comparing the 1982 and 1985
            cohorts   113
Fig. 8.3   Evaluation of course as satisfied/very satisfied   114
Fig. 8.4   Would do the same course again   115
Fig. 8.5   Value of degree course in employment: has been useful   116
Fig. 8.6   Value of degree course in employment: will be useful   116

Tab. 8.7   Do you consider that your experience in higher
           education helped you gain or improve any of the
           following abilities?   118
Tab. 8.8   Benefits of higher education: cohort comparisons   120
Fig. 8.9   Benefits of higher education: critical thinking   123
Fig. 8.10 Benefits of higher education: written communication   123
Fig. 8.11 Benefits of higher education: spoken communication   123
Fig. 8.12 Benefits of higher education: numeracy   123
Fig. 8.13 Benefits of higher education: leadership   125
Tab. 8.14 Role performance related benefits: top scorers   126
Tab. 8.15 The extent to which graduates feel they have had
           opportunities to develop transferable skills (after two
           years)   127
Tab. 8.16 Evaluation of work experience (WEX) 1982 and 1985
           panels   130
Fig. 8.17 Work experience benefits: all students 1985   132
Fig. 8.18 Work experience benefits (1985 panel): helped
           communication   132
Fig. 8.19 Work experience benefits (1985 panel): helped
           self-confidence   133
Fig. 8.20 Work experience benefits (1985 panel): helped
           problem solving   133
Fig. 8.21 Work experience benefits (1985 panel): helped
           commercial awareness   134
Fig. 8.22 Work experience benefits (1985 panel): helped
           numeracy   134
Fig. 8.23 Work experience benefits (1985 panel): helped
           leadership   135
Fig. 8.24 Work experience benefits (1985 panel): helped
           commitment to course work   135
Fig. 8.25 Work experience and job prospects: proportion
           perceiving benefits

Preface

Most higher education courses claim to be preparing their students for something – a job, a better life, personal fulfilment. It was a concern to examine the validity of such claims that led the Council for National Academic Awards (CNAA) to support studies of the experiences and views of graduates. The studies were conducted between 1983 and 1989 and took the form of longitudinal surveys of two large panels of graduates. In establishing these studies, the CNAA was reflecting the importance that had always been attached in the then polytechnic and college sector in the United Kingdom to undergraduate teaching and to the development of courses which, if not narrowly vocational in their aims, exhibited a strong emphasis on some kind of future utility.

Whether and how higher education courses prepare students for employment and enable graduates to obtain suitable, worthwhile and satisfying jobs is a central theme of this study. The intention of this book is to provide an analysis of some of the evidence collected. It is hoped that this will increase the understanding of the nature of the higher education and labour market relationship to the advantage of higher educational institutions and their students.

The data on which this book is based represent a valuable source of intelligence about the experiences of graduates and the relationship between higher education and the labour market. Collecting information in a policy climate characterised by rapid change is always frought with difficulty, however. During the period of the study, higher education underwent a series of major changes. The most important one from the point of view of the evidence presented in this book is the altered status of polytechnics. Since the study, all of these institutions have been granted university status and been brought into a system of funding and control shared with the traditional university sector. The effects of the abolition of the binary divide on the labour market relationships of students and courses lie in the future and need to be assessed by further research.

We would like to acknowledge the support and advice of the following: the members of the various CNAA committees which have had oversight of the project and, in particular, Professor Gareth

Williams, chairman of the former Higher Education and Work Project Committee; CNAA officers – Dr Alan Crispin, Dr Alison Baker and Mr Chris Boys; the Department of Social Sciences and the Computer Centre at South Bank Polytechnic; Professor David Jary, Dr David Gatley, Dr Tony Chapman and Mr Jim Zacune in the Department of Sociology at Staffordshire Polytechnic. We are especially grateful to Dr Paul Close of the University of Derby for his editorial assistance in preparing the final version of the manuscript. Finally, our thanks go to Ms Sian Dyer for typing this manuscript.

Chapter One

The Project

Introduction and Summary

Chapter One spells out the background context, guiding rationale, main aims and central concerns of the Higher Education and the Labour Market (HELM) project – the latest in a series of projects supported by the Council for National Academic Awards on the relationship between higher education and the labour market. This chapter outlines what previous research and current theory tell us – and do not tell us – about the higher education and the labour market relationship (the 'helm' relationship). It spotlights various doubts and deficiencies surrounding what is known and understood about the relationship.

The primary aim of the project has been to improve our understanding of the 'helm' relationship by generating and interpreting evidence about the 'higher education into employment' transition as experienced and viewed by graduates themselves. The principal purpose is to clarify the 'helm' relationship not just for its own sake or to improve theory, but in order to inform (a) student choices *vis-à-vis* careers and courses; (b) institutional course design and development; (c) social and educational (state) policy – especially in view of the state's increasing approach to higher education as the means for preparing skilled, 'competent' graduates judged in terms of the productive requirements and potential of the economy; and (d) in conjunction with economic processes and trends, employer recruitment strategies.

Thus, the primary aim and principal purpose of the HELM project can be summarised as follows:

to inform policy formation on the links between higher education and the labour market by looking at the experiences of graduates and examining the contribution of courses to career development.

The central, driving concerns of the project are (a) the 'extent to which higher education courses prepare students for employment'; (b) the 'extent to which courses enable graduates to obtain worthwhile and satisfying jobs'. An underlying theme of the project has been that the role of higher education in the successful transition of graduates to work is to some extent circumscribed by, on the one hand, the aspirations and characteristics of graduates themselves, and on the other the constraints imposed by a fluctuating labour market.

The Higher Education and the Labour Market Relationship

In this chapter, it is pointed out that the 'higher education into the labour market' transition can be partly – and perhaps increasingly – understood and assessed in terms of the way higher education courses are 'preparation for' the graduate labour market, and therefore the demands of employers and the needs of the economy with its various sectors and prevailing trends. It is argued that higher education courses have been increasingly judged, monitored and designed (influenced by a combination of changing economic needs and state policy) with reference to graduate 'competences' judged in terms of labour market, employment and career skills. The project set out to discover the kinds of jobs graduates from particular types of course get, and 'how far graduates themselves find that they possess the competences required by their jobs, and how far they feel that they obtained them in higher education'.

The intention has been to generate original evidence about several linked empirical issues:

(a) The character and importance within the 'helm' relationship of student choices, aspirations and demands *vis-à-vis* higher education courses, perhaps with subsequent labour market, employment and career considerations in mind. This issue can be summarised as being about relevance and importance of 'student orientations' towards the 'helm' relationship. The study recognises that student orientations will be far from unitary or static. They will originate within various and changing pre-course social circumstances; be differentially re-shaped under the influence of course experiences; and eventually emerge as a range of 'graduate orientations' towards the labour market, employment and careers.

(b) The way student orientations are not merely shaped by but also have a shaping effect on higher education courses and the 'helm' relationship. They will have an influence on the activities of course designers albeit alongside – and to some extent in competition with – influences stemming from both the state and the economy by way of employer orientations and demands.

(c) The implications for the 'helm' relationship of changes in labour market demand for graduates. Fluctuations in the demand for graduates, both qualitative and quantitative, are more important in their consequences for graduates from certain courses and subjects than others. Patterns of labour market segmentation, especially along gender lines, further influence the success of graduates in their search for work.

(d) The impact on the 'helm' relationship of differences in status and reputation of different sectors within the higher education system itself. The type of institution a student attends has labour market ramifications which, it could be argued, are unwarranted given the traditionally homogenous nature of higher education curricula and standards across the binary divide.

(e) The way student/graduate orientations shape and continue to be shaped by graduate experience within the labour market, employment and careers. Student orientations will help shape graduate employment experience and impressions, including the extent to which graduates view their higher education courses as having properly prepared them for the labour market, especially with reference to their 'competences' as employees. Any discrepancies between, on the one hand, student orientations and preparation and, on the other hand, employment demands and skill requirements are likely to feed into graduate impressions of and satisfactions about the 'helm' relationship.

The project is guided by the assumption that graduate experiences and impressions are a legitimate and highly instructive source of evidence about the 'helm' relationship.

There is a considerable amount of information about the higher education into employment transition of a quantitative kind – such as through the annual First Destinations Statistics (FDS) – but while their value is recognised, they provide only limited evidence about the quality of this transition. Moreover, while there is a lot of 'snap-shot' evidence (such as, again, through the FDS), the intention behind the project has been to uncover information of a longitudinal kind.

The study takes into account the possibility of a link between changes in student/graduate orientations, experiences and impressions over time and variations in these items stemming back to pre-course social circumstances and student/candidate characteristics. The possibility emerges of student graduate orientations, experiences and impressions *vis-à-vis* the 'helm' relationship becoming less and less unitary due to the effects of higher educational expansion and 'social catchment' alterations. Thus, in recent years, there has been a deliberate and concerted policy by the state and educational institutions to extend the 'social catchment' of higher education students in favour of those sections of society previously 'under-represented', including 'women, ethnic minorities and mature students'. It is recognised, however, that 'social class remains the largest factor associated with educational inequalities'.

A guiding task of the project has been to investigate and help unravel the 'interplay between educational qualifications and personal [social] characteristics in determining employment success'. The intention has been to gather and interpret evidence in conjunction with the development of an analytical model so as to clarify this interplay, while taking account of the influence of further intervening factors – such as institutional differences (including those to do with status and reputation) which may well be in the process of becoming greater due to, for instance, the new funding arrangements. Institutional status differences may have considerable consequences for the 'helm' relationship by virtue of the way they influence (a) student/candidate decisions and choices about institutions and courses and (b) employer choices within the graduate labour market.

Thus, the intention has been to develop an analytical model of the 'helm' relationship which takes full account of the 'interconnectedness between student characteristics, types of higher education and prospects in the labour market... in the several segmented markets to which graduates seek entry'. In a sense, this 'interconnectedness' is the major focus of the project.

The model for analyzing the 'helm' relationship in conjunction with the evidence about the relationship is developed in Chapter Three. This is preceded in Chapter Two by a description and explanation of the method, procedures and techniques used to gather the original survey evidence. In the remainder of this chapter, further detail is provided about the context of the project.

Graduate Destinations

The information contained in the following chapters was collected from graduates over a period of up to five years after their graduation. As such, it contrasts with the main public source of information about graduates' destinations, the annual First Destinations Statistics (FDS) organised by the careers services of higher education institutions and used in a variety of annual statistical publications on higher education. The FDS provide a 'snapshot' of what graduates are doing six months after graduation. It contains simple factual information about whether the graduates are in employment (or still in education or unemployed), the sort of job they are doing and with what kind of employer. The very high response rate which the FDS achieves in its annual census makes it a uniquely valuable tool for identifying labour market changes confronting new graduates. But there are important things the FDS do not show. It indicates nothing about the quality of jobs – about how far graduates are satisfied with and feel prepared for them. Six months is too early to evaluate graduates' success in the labour market. Some graduates will still be in full-time education and some will be 'taking time off' before applying for jobs.

The FDS were established by the higher education careers services to provide relatively rapid feedback about what had happened during the preceding annual recruitment cycle. Over the period of the 1980s, the FDS destinations data became of increasing interest to national and institutional policy makers. With new forms of government interest in higher education, criteria by which to evaluate courses and institutions were sought which went beyond the internal consensus of the academic peer community. The 1987 White Paper spoke of the need to measure quality in terms of the achievements of students, educationally and in employment. The long list of performance indicators published by the CVCP contained graduate destinations (after five years as well as the six months survey) as part of the rather shorter list of indicators which had identifiable links to the educational process. Recognising the growing interest in quantitative performance data, the CNAA developed a Students Database to provide its institutions with a flexible and simple means for comparing their own performance against national student data, of which destination data from the FDS formed a central part.

As interest grows in the use of quantitative data to support the evaluation, planning and funding of higher education, the need for more longitudinal data has become apparent. All the CNAA supported projects on the 'helm' relationship have shown the great variability between students, courses and different types of jobs in both speed and structure of the transition to work. This variability can only be established and analysed through a more focused and selective approach to the study of the relationship between higher education and employment. The evidence reported in subsequent chapters points to the importance of continuing to collect data which allows for the study of graduate destinations over time as well as over different labour markets. Before the FDS can satisfactorily be used as a performance indicator of graduate entry to the labour market, more needs to be understood about the complex set of interactions between student choices and aspirations and labour market needs and demands which lead to the situation where some graduates walk straight into full time work, whereas others choose to remain in education or enter more marginal employment.

The Policy Context

Government policy on higher education has increasingly emphasised instrumental purposes, of which preparing a highly skilled labour force is a prime one. Questions about the relationship between higher education and the labour market are therefore raised with new force and in new forms. In the early part of the 1980s, concern was directed at graduate unemployment, which for some subject areas appeared high in the six months destinations survey. Our own earlier work indicated that unemployment did not persist for very long (Brennan and McGeevor, 1988), and subsequently a more buoyant labour market coupled with a projected demographic downturn in student numbers for the 1990s shifted the policy concern away from unemployment towards a fear of graduate shortages. The recession of the early nineties has swung concern back towards unemployment.

In a speech in Lancaster in January 1989 calling for a virtual doubling of student numbers in higher education, the Secretary of State for Education appeared to affirm the belief in what has been called the 'human capital approach' to higher education. This assumes that people are productive resources and that highly educated people are more productive than others. In other words, it assumes a relationship between investment in education and economic growth, for both the state and the individual, at least in the long term.

While the human capital approach remains influential, it is regarded with more reservations than it was during the 1960s period of educational expansion. Many of the reservations inform this report. Here we will consider two which relate closely to prevailing policy concerns.

Further expansion of higher education is held to be dependent upon extending access to sections of society currently under-represented. Women, ethnic minorities and mature students are the most frequently mentioned in this context, although social class remains the principal factor associated with educational inequalities. Extending access to higher education for these people is viewed both as a way of broadening social and occupational opportunities for the individuals concerned and as a means for increasing the supply of suitably qualified entrants into industry and the professions. This begs the question of the value of educational qualifications within the labour market when they are decoupled from the kinds of personal and social attributes which graduates have traditionally possessed. If, as has been suggested (Roizen and Jepson, 1985), employers are interested in qualifications on the grounds, not so much of them being indicative of the possession of relevant knowledge and skills, as of them being useful as a 'screen' for filtering the socially acceptable, then extending educational opportunities may not lead to extended employment opportunities. The interplay between educational qualifications and social characteristics in determining employment success is a central theme of this report (see Chapter Three).

A second but related reservation about human capital theory concerns the extent to which the highly educated can genuinely be regarded as highly productive. Much has been written on this issue, but simple conclusions are elusive. What is clear is that government no longer regards higher education as an unconditional good. Coupled with the commitment to extend access is a concern to improve the employment related skills of graduates. The Enterprise Initiative of the Training Agency is but the largest and best known of several recent developments which aim to improve the 'competences' of British graduates. Other initiatives include the Education for Capability project sponsored by the Royal Society for Arts, and the Employment of Humanities Graduates project which is but one of several CNAA activities (see Chapter Eight).

The graduates in the HELM project panels had completed their higher education before any of the above initiatives could take effect. Nevertheless, the thinking underlying them has long been a part of higher educational institutions (Silver and Brennan, 1988), particularly in the public sector. Many degree courses have been designed with the production of competent professionals as their overriding aim. Even where other educational aims have claimed priority, academics have been quick to see a serendipitous connection between educational and employment competences (Boys *et al.* 1988). Thus, a major theme of this report is how far graduates themselves find that they possess the competences required by their jobs, and how far they feel that they obtained them in higher education (see Chapter Eight).

Higher Education Institutions

If accountability, access and competency are key words in current United Kingdom higher education policy, they assume different force and significance in different parts of the system. Higher education in the UK – even if narrowly defined in terms of undergraduate teaching

– takes place in well over a hundred separate institutions. This report is concerned primarily with those institutions which until recently offered courses leading to CNAA awards – more than half the total of institutions and slightly over a third of the total number of students. But CNAA courses need to be seen in a wider context, covering the works not only of universities but also of the various diploma and sub-degree courses, especially those leading to the awards of the Business and Technician Education Council (BTEC). University and BTEC students are represented in the HELM graduate surveys, and a few preliminary comments about the institutional shape of British higher education is useful at this point.

The familiarity of the now changing binary divide can both exaggerate and disguise the extent of institutional differences. Compared with many systems of higher education, the UK system is remarkably homogeneous. Most students take three or four year courses leading to a bachelor's degree which is formally equivalent in standard irrespective of the institution attended. Entry qualifications are also formally equivalent as are the arrangements for students' financial support. Curricular differences exist and should not be underestimated, but they do not align with a neat differentiation of institutional types. The polytechnics are far from being the vocational, technical institutions to be found among their continental counterparts. Higher education in the UK has been described as a relatively 'flat hierarchy' with only small differences between institutions.

How do these system characteristics affect the direction and consequences of current policies? Notwithstanding the formal equivalence of academic awards, there are clear differences in social status and academic reputation between institutions, both within and between the two sectors of the binary divide. The persistence in popular perceptions of such a divide is evidenced by a new language of status differentials in references to 'new' and 'old' universities. If the system is to grow towards mass higher education, it seems likely that institutional differences will increase with differing institutional locations, profiles of student intake, and course provisions. There are signs of this in the new funding arrangements, particularly in the university sector where formal rankings of departments (and hence informal rankings of institutions) have become the norm. Institutional differentiation is one way in which expanded systems of higher education can continue to fulfil the disparate functions of elite higher education together with some new ones.

Put another way, students at the beginning of the 1990s face an unparalleled choice of institutions and courses. Not all courses and institutions have the same outcomes; and not all students have very much choice in practice. In short, there is an intimate interconnectedness between student characteristics, types of higher education and graduate prospects in the labour market, or more precisely in the several segments of the labour market to which graduates seek entry. It is this interconnectedness which is the central focus of the HELM project.

This Book

This book is the latest to emerge as a result of CNAA commissioned studies about the higher education and the labour market relationship. Earlier projects include a study of institutional responsiveness to labour market pressures (Boys *et al.* 1988) and a study of the vocational aims of higher education courses (Silver and Brennan 1988). The immediate antecedent of the HELM project is a study of the employment experiences of a panel of CNAA graduates from the 1982 national cohort over their first three years in the labour market (Brennan and McGeevor 1988). Further information collected from this panel along with an entirely fresh panel drawn from the 1985 national cohort of graduates provides the basis for this book.

The general rationale for the HELM project has been to inform policy formation on the links between higher education and the labour market by looking at the experiences of graduates and examining the contribution of courses to career development. The project was undertaken and this book has been written in the belief that knowledge of the 'qualities' and experiences of graduates can be used not only to inform strategic planning decisions faced by institutions and national planning bodies, but also to contribute to the design and evaluation of courses and to assist students in their decisions and choices about courses and employment.

The next chapter presents details of HELM's graduate samples and empirical investigation. Here it is sufficient to note the point that the whole of the book builds on previous work by examining the experiences of graduates under differing labour market conditions; CNAA graduates in comparison with university graduates and BTEC diplomates; and the more recent career experience of our original 1982 graduate panel.

Chapters Three and Four lay the foundation of the discussion and analysis running through the remainder of the book. Chapter Three develops a model for analysing the interconnectedness between students, higher education and the labour market. The chapter also examines the variety both of the employment-related course aims and of the employment-related student characteristics, orientations and aspirations. Chapter Four considers some of the main features of a changing graduate labour market and the implications of these changes for patterns of graduate recruitment.

Chapter Five moves on to consider the changes taking place within the labour market and addresses the issue of whether certain types of student, course and institution are more affected than others by labour market fluctuations. This involves a comparison of the experiences of the graduates in the 1982 and 1985 panels. It is recognised that 1982 was an especially difficult year for graduate opportunities for entry into the labour market, but that by 1985 the situation had improved considerably. Chapter Five examines the implications of the anticipated 'shortage' of graduates – especially within certain segments of the labour market – during the 1990s.

Chapter Six provides a closer examination of the spread of graduate destinations, and includes an attempt to identify those student and course characteristics which are associated with long-term success within the labour market. In Chapter Seven we look at institutional and qualification (CNAA degree, university degree, BTEC Higher National Diploma) differences in relation to labour market entry and employment opportunities. Chapter Eight is concerned with the graduates' own conceptions of employment-related competences. We examine how far 'competences' are perceived to be transferable both between higher education and employment. We also consider the contribution of 'in-service' experience – through, for instance, sandwich courses – to the development of work-related competences. Finally, Chapter Nine draws out some overall conclusions along with the policy implications of the project's findings.

Chapter Two

The Research

Introduction and Summary

The research strategy centred on obtaining empirical evidence through the use of survey questionnaires designed to allow two panels of graduates to record their experiences and impressions. The first panel was selected from the 1982 cohort of graduates, the second from 1985. The 1982 panel was 'inherited' from the previous CNAA study (Brennan and McGeevor, 1988).

The HELM 1985 graduate panel survey was designed with several aims in mind. First, information should be collected to enable an examination of the employment status two years into employment of 1985 graduates from a wide selection of CNAA courses. The cohort panel would be drawn in such a way as to enable meaningful comparisons with that of the previously surveyed cohort of 1982. Second, in order to establish whether there is an institutional effect on the employment of graduates, comparison of the employment experiences of CNAA graduates with those of university graduates from equivalent courses was seen to be a major requirement, and accordingly smaller samples of university courses and graduates in selected subject types were drawn. Such comparisons were made for the 1982 cohort between polytechnic and college graduates. Some comparisons were to be made also with BTEC students. Third, information gained from graduates a few years into employment would be analysed in relation to the evidence provided by the annual first destination statistics.

The survey questionnaires were targeted at collecting the following range of evidence:

(i) graduates' labour market and employment experiences in relation to their higher education background, orientations, choices and retrospective impressions;

(ii) graduates' careers and experiences with regard to not only employment, but also unemployment and further study;

(iii) information which allows comparisons between students with differing higher educational backgrounds judged with reference to such matters as subject area, course type, qualification type and institution type;

(iv) information which allows comparisons over time – longitudinal enquiries;

(v) information which allows comparisons between panels of graduates from difference national cohorts;

(vi) information which allows comparisons between students and courses by social background – by 'social catchment'.

This chapter details the procedure by which the panels of students investigated were selected in accordance with the emphasis in the project on the way, not students as such, but higher education *courses* relate to the labour market. The procedure entailed a process of identification and selection of 'subject areas' (such as accountancy and mechanical engineering); 'course types' (distinguished according to the extent of their 'vocational' preparation); 'qualification types' (covering CNAA degrees, university degrees, BTEC Higher National Diplomas); and 'institution types' (covering polytechnics, universities and colleges/institutes of higher education).

We approach these aims with varying degrees of confidence. Whereas we feel some confidence about discussing differences between course types and student types, we feel less confident about making comparisons over time. Both the courses and the sample targeted have changed. The comparisons between courses across the binary divide are based on a matching of these courses, but some caution is necessary. The outcome is a comprehensive body of evidence enabling the analysis of various aspects of the 'helm' relationship in the rest of this report, beginning in Chapter Three with the development of a general analytical model. As analysis of the more general factors that enter into the 'helm' relationship constitutes the main focus of this book, detailed interpretation of the labour market experiences of graduates from individual subject areas has not been attempted.

The Course Samples

The 1982 panel was based on a ten per cent sample drawn from the national CNAA graduate cohort of that year. The aim of the original survey was to examine the employment outcomes of CNAA courses in relation to course objectives. An early conceptualisation by the researchers based on the vocational intent of degree courses was used in selecting the 31 course types represented in the course type sample (for details see Brennan and McGeevor, 1988). The sample of course types was selected from the complete range of full-time CNAA polytechnic and college undergraduate provision, and was drawn from 33 public sector institutions chosen on the basis of geographical spread and institutional type. Course types were selected in order to explore different forms of relationship between degree qualifications and jobs, and the criteria for selection included subject field, curriculum organisation, course objectives and size of enrolments. Individual courses were selected as typical of the course type (following inspection of prospectuses and consultation with CNAA subject board secretaries and members) and in order to obtain a good geographical and institutional spread. For each course type, the aim was to obtain a sample of at least a hundred graduates.

Similar criteria were followed in selecting the 1985 panel. A first criterion was to provide continuity with the 1982 sample of full-time courses, while responding to some of the theoretical and policy issues raised by the earlier survey. A smaller number of course types was chosen, 24 in all. Some course types in the 1982 sample were left out of the 1985 sample – an example being pharmacy. A few course types were included in the 1985 sample that did not appear in the 1982 sample – one example being creative and performing arts. It was intended that the sample would broadly represent the subject balance in higher education; would take account of special interests identified by CNAA committees; and would include course types with more than 500 graduates overall. Particular course types would be comparable with or 'matched' to those to be selected from universities to enable comparisons on a range of variables. Courses were chosen only if they represented 'main stream' examples of the course type. A list of course types in each of the 1982 and 1985 samples is presented in Table 2.1.

Table 2.1: Helm project course types

1982 CNAA	1985 CNAA
Accountancy	Accountancy
	Architecture
Biology	Biology
Business Studies	Business Studies
Chemistry	
Civil Engineering	
	Combined Studies
Communication Studies	Communication Studies
Computer Science	Computer Science
	Creative & Performing Arts

Table 2.1: Helm project course types (continued)

Economics	Economics
	Education
Electrical Engineering	Electrical Engineering
English Literature	
Environmental Planning	
Environmental Science	
Estate Management	Estate Management
Fine Art	Fine Art
Geography	
Graphic Design	Graphic Design
Hotel and Catering Management	
Humanities	Humanities
Interfaculty	
Law	Law
Librarianship	
Mathematics	
	Mechanical Engineering
Modern Languages	Modern Languages
	Quantity Surveying
Nursing	
Science (combined)	Science (combined)
Social Science	Social Science
	Sport and Recreation Management
Pharmacy	
Production Engineering	
Psychology	
Textile and Fashion Design	Textile and Fashion Design
Three Dimensional Design	Three Dimensional Design

University
Accountancy
Biology
Computing
Economics
History/English
Mechanical Engineering

BTEC
Business Studies
Computing
Mechanical Engineering

For polytechnics and colleges, individual institutions running a course identified through the structure of the quota selection of courses outlined above were included in the survey. For universities, a list of the institutions which run similar courses was treated as a sampling frame from which institutions were selected. In view of the co-operation received from institutions and the need to guarantee institutional anonymity, a list of institutions in the samples has not been included in the report.

The 1985 sample differs from the 1982 sample in that equal numbers of male and female graduates were sought for each course – 150 male and 150 female. For each course we aimed for 300 graduates irrespective of whether it was in a high or low enrolment field. Given the skewed gender distribution on some courses, it was not always possible to get equal numbers of male and female graduates on all courses. Whenever aggregate analysis has been done, the 1985 sample has been weighted to take account of gender.

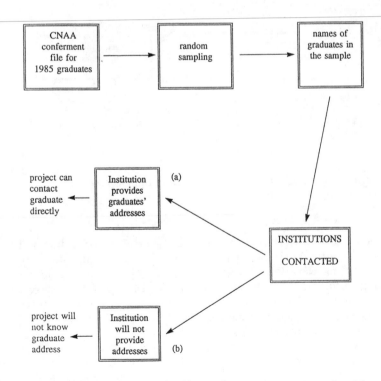

Figure 2.2a: Polytechnics and colleges – how contact was made with the 1985 panel

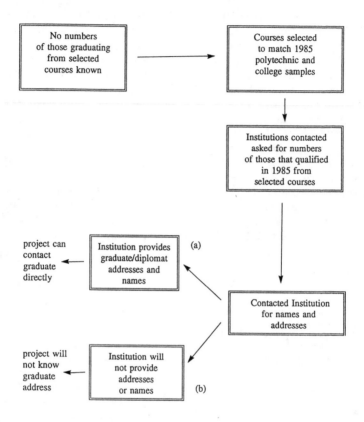

Figure 2.2b: BTEC and university graduates in 1985 panel

Both cohort panels were selected in order to explore relationships and do not purport to be fully representative of all CNAA and university graduates. Nevertheless, they broadly reflect the numbers graduating in the main faculty areas, as indicated by the CNAA subject committee structure existing at the start of the project. The courses have been selected as representative of the range of courses found within these faculty areas.

Table 2.3: Response rate of the 1982 panel

COURSE TYPE	A	B	C	D	E	F	G	H
HUMANITIES	246	164	67%	117	48%	95	39%	58%
ENGLISH LITERATURE	89	56	63%	32	36%	29	33%	52%
GEOGRAPHY	114	89	78%	63	55%	66	58%	74%
MODERN LANGUAGES	111	85	77%	61	55%	50	45%	59%
LIBRARIANSHIP	141	101	72%	84	60%	64	45%	59%
COMMUNICATION STUDIES	133	96	72%	60	45%	41	31%	43%
ACCOUNTANCY	99	52	53%	34	34%	30	30%	58%
BUSINESS STUDIES	153	105	69%	76	50%	50	33%	48%
ECONOMICS	101	54	53%	33	33%	27	27%	50%
LAW	133	57	43%	33	25%	23	17%	40%
PSYCHOLOGY	119	83	70%	65	55%	48	40%	58%
SOCIAL STUDIES	187	122	85%	84	45%	65	35%	53%
ENVIRONMENTAL PLANNING	94	63	67%	50	53%	37	39%	59%
URBAN ESTATE MANAGEMENT	115	82	71%	47	41%	45	39%	55%
CIVIL ENGINEERING	106	66	62%	53	50%	42	40%	64%
ELECTRICAL ENGINEERING	78	53	68%	31	40%	17	22%	32%
PRODUCTION ENGINEERING	102	55	54%	42	41%	35	34%	64%
MATHS	73	54	74%	33	45%	35	48%	85%
HOTEL & CATERING ADMINISTRATION	113	72	64%	59	52%	45	40%	63%
SCIENCE	251	143	57%	99	39%	68	27%	48%
APPLIED CHEMISTRY	106	73	69%	52	49%	43	41%	59%
APPLIED BIOLOGY	173	135	78%	99	57%	74	43%	55%
PHARMACY	123	83	67%	46	37%	33	27%	40%
NURSING	74	65	88%	49	66%	52	70%	80%
COMPUTER SCIENCE	89	54	61%	41	46%	38	43%	70%
ENVIRONMENTAL SCIENCE	108	85	79%	54	50%	49	45%	58%
FINE ART	123	72	59%	44	36%	37	30%	51%
GRAPHIC DESIGN	172	95	55%	67	39%	45	26%	47%
TEXTILE & FASHION DESIGN	141	87	62%	44	31%	45	32%	52%
3D DESIGN	134	83	62%	54	40%	32	24%	39%
INTERFACULTY	231	151	65%	119	52%	78	34%	52%
HUMANITIES	246	164	67%	117	48%	95	39%	58%
ENGLISH LITERATURE	89	56	63%	32	36%	29	33%	52%
ALL COURSES	4016	2635	66%	1826	45%	1451	36%	55%

A = Original list of graduates   B = Number of replies to 1983 questionnaire
C = B as a percentage of A   D = Number of replies to 1984 questionnaire
E = D as a percentage of A   F = Number of replies to 1985 questionnaire
G = F as a percentage of A
H = F as a percentage of B

Table 2.4: Response rate of the 1985 panel

COURSE	TARGET AIMED AT CONTAC TING	TOTAL RESPONSE	% RESPONSE LARGE QUESTIONN -AIRES	SHORT QUEST IONN- AIRES	TOTAL	OVERALL TOTAL%
CNAA GRADUATES						
Accountancy	301	132	43.9%	40	172	57.1%
Architecture	302	105	34.8%	46	151	50.0%
Biology	300	173	57.7%	33	206	68.7%
Business	229	135	59.0%	33	168	73.4%
Combined Studies	297	138	46.5%	28	166	55.9%
Communications	178	81	45.5%	19	100	56.2%
Computing	299	148	49.5%	32	180	60.2%
Perf Arts	304	122	40.1%	25	147	48.4%
Est Mngment	304	149	49.0%	35	184	60.5%
Economics	311	119	38.3%	28	147	47.3%
Education	300	189	63.0%	23	212	70.7%
Elec Engineering	300	140	46.7%	25	165	55.0%
Fine Art	280	84	30.0%	28	112	40.0%
Graph Design	299	100	33.4%	30	130	43.5%
Humanities	300	91	30.3%	30	121	40.3%
Law	290	127	43.8%	35	162	55.9%
Mechan Eng	291	109	37.5%	19	128	44.0%
Mod Lang	300	127	42.3%	35	162	54.0%
Quant Surveying	300	105	35.0%	34	139	46.3%
Science	219	105	47.9%	17	122	55.7%
Social Science	300	118	39.3%	28	146	48.7%
Sport/Recreation	300	143	47.7%	48	191	63.7%
Textile/Fashion	299	109	36.5%	36	145	48.5%
3D Design	300	101	33.7%	29	130	43.3%
TOTAL	6903	2950	42.7%	736	386	53.4%

Table 2.4: Response rate of the 1985 panel (continued)

COURSE	TARGET AIMED AT CONTAC TING	TOTAL RESPONSE	% RESPONSE LARGE QUESTIONN -AIRES	SHORT QUEST IONN- AIRES	TOTAL	OVERALL TOTAL%
UNIVERSITY GRADUATES						
U Account	207	78	37.7%	12	90	43.5%
U Biology	150	76	50.7%	12	88	58.7%
U Computing	162	74	45.7%	12	86	53.1%
U Economics	238	109	45.8%	18	127	53.4%
U Humanities	615	297	48.3%	59	356	57.9%
U Mech Eng	237	102	43.0%	13	115	48.5%
TOTAL	1687	736	43.6%	126	862	51.1%
BTEC DIPLOMATES						
BT Business	315	129	41.0%	7	136	43.2%
BT Computing	299	137	45.8%	8	145	48.5%
BT Mechanical	145	80	55.2%	2	82	56.6%
TOTAL	759	346	45.6%	17	363	47.8%

The Selection of Graduates

The sampling frame for each course in polytechnics was the name list of the 1985 graduates for that course made available through the CNAA conferment files. Addresses of students were obtained through the institutions. In the case of universities, where numbers graduating from selected courses were not known, institutions provided the numbers and addresses of the graduates. The questionnaires were sent out to students either through institutions or directly from the project centre, depending on whether the institutions agreed to pass on an address list. For a detailed outline of how contact was made with the samples, see Figure 2.2.

Each sample was contacted several times (the 1982 sample in 1983, 1984, 1985 and 1988; and the 1985 sample in 1987 and 1988) giving rise to differing response rates on different occasions. This is an important consideration when interpreting the data. It is to be expected in longitudinal surveys that later replies will show reduced rates of panel participation. For detailed information about the response rates, see Tables 2.3. and 2.4. Following completion of the project, CNAA collected further data from both samples during 1990. These recent data have not been used in the preparation of this report. Subsequent reports will incorporate the findings of this latest data.

Cohort Comparisons

With each panel of graduates being sent questionnaires at several different points in time, the data collected allow for cohort comparisons. In addition, the possibilities for comparing the two panels across time can be seen in Figure 2.5. Wave Two of the 1982 panel is directly comparable with Wave One of the 1985 panel because each is two years after graduation. Various comparisons will be made throughout the report between the changing employment destinations and labour market conditions of each panel at similar points in time in its progression into employment. Comparisons will be made between panels on the profiles of their career progression over time with regard to, for instance, speed and pattern of employment entry over the first three years, while paying special attention to the number of job changes in the first years after graduation. Each chapter of this report will approach the longitudinal aspect of this project in a way appropriate to its particular topic of interest.

Figure 2.5: Contact points with the two graduate panels

WAVE 1	WAVE 2	WAVE 3	WAVE 4
1982 Panel			
Contacted in 1983 1 year after graduation	Contacted in 1984 2 years after graduation	Contacted in 1985 3 years after graduation	Contacted in 1988 4 years after graduation
1985 Panel			
Contacted in 1987 2 years after graduation	Contacted in 1988 3 years after graduation		

The Questionnaires

The graduates were asked a range of questions in the targeted areas outlined above. The topics covered by the questionnaires are those of early education; reasons for degree choice; perceived purposes and benefits of the higher education experience; detailed information about employment conditions since graduation; and further study and training. Many questions were repeated between the two panels and over the several waves of the study. The 1985 questionnaires are presented in the appendix.

The richness of the data collected permits a great deal more analysis than this book is able to present, and it is hoped that the information will be used in other contexts and for further analytical policy and practical purposes.

Students and Courses into Employment

Introduction and Summary

Chapter One states that a central concern of the project is with how well higher education courses prepare students for the graduate labour market, employment and careers, given variations in the demand for graduates between labour market sectors and according to prevailing economic conditions.

Chapter Three develops a model for analysing the 'helm' relationship centred on the 'higher education into employment' transition and subsequent career as experienced and viewed by graduates themselves. The analytical model takes into account the way in which HELM project survey data both broadly confirm and complement previous evidence. It is abundantly clear that there is a strong relationship between the character of graduate entry into the labour market (and subsequent labour market careers and experiences) and the character of higher education courses (distinguished in terms of such matters as subject area, course type, institution type and qualification type). It is also clear that there is a strong relationship between, on the one hand, student orientations and course type distinguished in terms of the extent of their vocational associations and, on the other hand, subsequent graduate labour market experiences.

Moreover, the evidence suggests that because there is a strong relationship between student orientation and student social circumstances and characteristics – student 'social profile' – there is also a strong relationship between student social profile and eventual labour market experiences. The student social circumstances and characteristics which appear foremost in influencing student orientation, choice of higher education courses and thereby graduate labour market entry, career and experiences include previous educational experience, social class, gender, age and ethnicity.

This chapter, in developing a model for the analysis of the 'helm' relationship, takes into account and elucidates the strength of the links between student social profile, student course and career orientation, course of study and graduate labour market experiences. The model treats higher education courses as occupying an intermediary – albeit somewhat independently influential – location between two markets. That is, higher education courses mediate between a student/candidate market prior to higher education course entry and a graduate labour market following higher education. In this way, higher education courses bring into contact, on the one hand, student social profiles, orientations and demands (with regard to courses and careers) and, on the other hand, employer demands and economic requirements with regard to graduate skills and competences.

At the same time, the model acknowledges the way higher education courses themselves have both a shaping influence on student/graduate orientations, expectations and demands and a preparatory influence on student/graduate skills and competences. In this way, not only prior social circumstances and characteristics, but also higher education courses, help account for the extent to which there is a match between (a) student/graduate orientations, expectations, demands, preparedness and competences and (b) labour market, employment and career demands placed on and experienced by graduates. Accordingly, students' labour market and employment satisfaction will be reflected in their retrospective impressions of their higher education courses, and in particular of whether and to what extent their higher education courses prepared them appropriately and adequately for graduate labour market, employment and career demands.

While higher education courses have an independent influence on student/graduate orientations, demands and satisfaction, in turn they will themselves be shaped by influences stemming from both the student/candidate market and the graduate labour market, where in each case the shaping influences involved will operate by way of course development and design considerations, concerns and constraints. The issue arises of the relative weight which each of the two markets does, might and should have on course development and design. Chapter Three deals with this issue by according special importance to student orientations (distinguished in terms of the extent to which they are vocationally, instrumentally and extrinsically inclined) in the context of (a) variations in student social profiles and (b) social and economic change.

It is argued that it is important to recognise how, in the first place, many students are not vocationally orientated in their decisions to enter higher education and in their choices of particular higher education courses; and connected with this, that many students have far from a purely instrumental and extrinsic approach to higher education. Moreover, the vocational approach among students may be relatively speaking on the decline following the inter-play of, in particular, two concurrent developments: (a) the expansion of higher education and associated increase in student places; and (b) the demographic decline in the proportion and availability of school-leavers.

These developments have been accompanied by an alteration in the social profile of students in that there has been an increase in higher educational demand for and entry of older, mature students – and especially of mature female students. Such students, it is argued, tend to have orientations towards higher education which differ from those of younger – especially younger male – students. That is, both mature and female students are less likely than either young or male students to have a purely career orientated approach to higher education.

The argument pays due attention to the broader social and economic ramifications of this trend in student social catchment and orientations by recognising (a) the issue of, and influencing factors behind, supply in the student/candidate market; and connected to this (b) the issue of the relationship between (i) the increase in mature and female students along with their more non-vocational student orientation and (ii) changes in such matters as employer demand, economic requirements and occupational conditions and characteristics. Essentially, current and prospective economic development is likely to encourage changes in employment needs and employer demands in relation to graduates – their skills, competences and preparation – and so in relation to higher education course design. However, it is crucial for both employers and course designers to acknowledge and accommodate the various, complex and evolving student (candidate/graduate) orientations to courses and careers, and the way these orientations are dependent upon the changing social catchments, characteristics and backgrounds of students.

Employers and course designers need to recognise the full implications of the fact that the 'process by which graduate jobs get filled starts well before entry in higher education'; and that consequently – and crucially 'policies designed to meet changing labour power demands will not be successful unless closer attention is paid to the orientations of students entering higher education'.

The Model

During the last few years, a great deal of detailed research has been undertaken on the relationship between the nature of the degree course undertaken by a student and the entry of that student to the labour market. The research has shown, and as we shall see continues to show, a strong relationship between choice of degree subject and early employment status. Models of the nature of this relationship have been developed indicating how different types of courses are designed to relate to different types of labour markets (Brennan and McGeevor, 1988; Silver and Brennan, 1988). Some of these graduate labour markets are specialised, demanding particular types of educational qualifications, whilst others are more diffuse offering occupational opportunities to graduates from a wide variety of course backgrounds. The labour market for graduates is structured into different levels and sectors of jobs, each more or less secure and well paid, more or less open to graduates without particular sets of qualifications. Some parts of the labour market recruit virtually any type of graduate, recruitment to other parts is more or less regulated by formal and specialised qualification requirements. Though it seems generally expected that the demand for higher education is expected to grow over the next decades, as is employer demand for graduates, there will continue to be considerable variations between different fields of both courses and employment. Moreover, there is likely to continue to be some subjects and courses, and some employment sectors, with greater recruitment difficulties than others.

It is also evident that students themselves do not express a uniform demand for particular types of courses or careers. Students enter higher education with a wide range of goals in mind, only some of which relate to the pursuit of economic and vocational success. Indeed for some students the higher education experience is as much about discovering a commitment to a vocation as about pursuing one. The social demand for higher education is ultimately determined by individual decisions about what subject to study, decisions aggregated to express a collective demand. The attitudes and expectations that enter into those decisions are complex and difficult to disentangle. The process by which graduate jobs get filled starts well before entry to higher education. The choice of which higher education institution to apply for and course to follow is in itself the outcome of a long process of decision making, reflecting different occupational orientations and expectations determined by a combination of personal interest and socio-economic circumstances, along with the power of accumulated credentials to limit or extend educational opportunities. Courses differ in that they attract, as well as graduate,

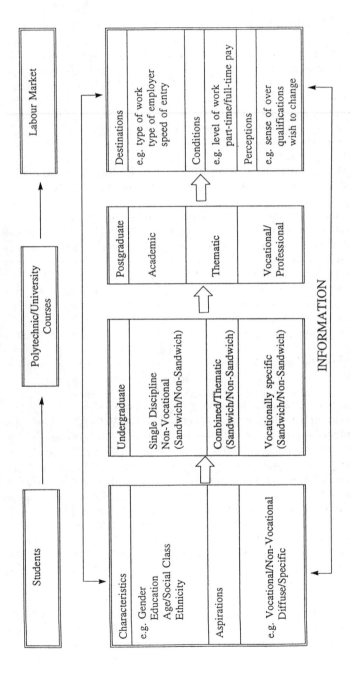

Figure 3.1: Students and courses in employment: an interactive model

students with different kinds of occupational orientations and aspirations.

As the nature of the chosen course structures students' subsequent entry to the labour market, the different aspirations students bring to courses become an important variable to consider in the development of a model of graduate labour market entry. With two such complex and heterogeneous markets interacting as that of students and that of highly skilled jobs, the task of 'matching' graduates with jobs lies at the heart of issues concerning the role of degree courses in labour market recruitment.

We can schematically present this complex relationship between students, courses and the labour market in a simple model (see Figure 3.1).

The aspirations of students, determined in part by their background, get channelled through course choice into different sectors and levels of the labour market. At each stage of this process, decisions are made in the light of information about the labour market fed back to students and course designers through information sources such as careers officers, the press and family contacts. In a system of perfect, up-to-date information and financially 'rational' choice, student aspirations should shift between courses in line with labour shortages and salary differentials. In the real and more complex world of educational and career choice, however, decisions are made in the light of much wider considerations of social and personal motivations and expectations towards the value and uses of higher education. With enrolment relying on student demand for places, as well as on central control through funding mechanisms, the expansion in higher education has to serve dual functions: that of meeting students' aspirations and that of providing the relevant skills for the changing needs of the labour market. These functions are not always in harmony, which sets one of the frameworks for present debates about the role of higher education in society in general and in the economy.

In this chapter we will look a little further into factors affecting the input of students into higher education that are of relevance to later careers in the labour market. We will do this in order to establish important course differences, along with the relationship of such differences to what can be called the 'social catchment' of a particular type of course. The aim is to provide a background against which the early career destinations of graduates can be understood, and the data will be used to characterise courses, not to give an overall picture of the student population as a whole. It is our belief that policies designed to meet changing labour power demands will not be successful unless closer attention is paid to the orientations of students entering higher education.

Access and Higher Education

In the present climate of expansion in higher education, the question of access has become a major policy issue. It has two dimensions: first, an increase in the number of places available to potential students on a wider range of courses, and second, the fostering of a motivation to further study on the part of individuals from a wider range of social and educational backgrounds than is at present the case. The total number of graduates is expected to grow, as is the demand from employers for graduates. An increase in the supply of places matched by a growth in the number of students is expected to lead to the satisfaction of the growing demand for skilled graduate labour in the economy. The hope, as expressed in a recent report on access, is that the 'universal aspiration for a home and a car will come to be matched by a common desire for a college education' (Ball, 1989).

The desire for higher education is not, however, a uniform wish for a unitary product. With both students and courses differing considerably as regards vocational relevance and the aims of further study, the notion of a supply of graduates to the labour market needs to be broken down for a greater understanding of what makes particular types of students choose particular types of courses, with consequent effects on their subsequent careers. The market of potential students is as complex and heterogenous as the market of jobs into which they are expected to slot as graduates. With the decline in school leaver cohorts and the growth in student numbers expected to encompass sectors of the population not previously the recipients of higher education, it is anticipated that there will continue to be considerable variations in both supply and demand between different fields of higher education and the labour market. If the purchasing power of students is given greater prominence, the problems raised by the need to match student aspirations with the balance of places provided in different disciplines and on different types of courses will necessitate an even closer look at student aspirations and their role in the process of admissions and recruitment to higher education.

Entry to higher education is not a straightforward process and there is no open access to higher education. The constraints on access, and hence on the number of students that eventually gain a place on a course, relate to several aspects of the recruitment process: the supply of places; institutional standards; previous education qualifications; student career preferences and course perceptions; and career opportunities and rewards. It is both a competitive system, where courses and institutions in high demand can set higher entry qualifications, and a selective system, where academics, professional, vocational organisations and internal financial bureaucratic structures can determine the nature of the student intake to each course. As there are no shared minimum admissions standards, courses can vary considerably in their openness and accessibility to potential students. This in practice also means that individual courses in high demand may have to develop course specific recruitment policies if they are to accommodate non-standard entrants and achieve institutional policies for extending access. This not only affects the overall A-level standards of a student body, but also more specific demands for particular types of pre-qualifications, such as GCSE Maths or English. The difference that A-level qualifications make to patterns of entry into higher education is shown by a recent OPCS study of factors affecting the demand for higher education for 17 to 20 year olds. The better the A-level result, the more the chance of being accepted by a university and the more chance a student has of gaining the place on the course and the institutions of his or her first choice. Related to this is the fact that pupils from independent schools and those who took at least one physical science A-level subject had higher average A-level scores than those taking a social science subject, who in turn had higher A-level scores than those taking an A-level in Arts (Redpath and Harvey, 1987).

Some courses protected by professional organisations with an interest in maintaining high entry standards and a strong market position, may find themselves in greater difficulties when it comes to a more open recruitment of candidates with non-standard qualifications. Faced with an increased demand and a funding system that favours the size rather than the quality of enrolment, pressures will be on courses to expand and accommodate less academically qualified students. A variety of study skills based access courses has been fostered with the aim of allowing alternative and competitive equivalents to A-level courses. However, by their very nature, such courses are easier to mount in the humanities and social sciences, and hence they do not go far in a major way to widen entry opportunities across the board. Indeed, they can be regarded as channelling certain kinds of student into certain kinds of course and thereby influencing in the long term the labour market relations of both courses and students.

Similarly, because of the differing nature of course provisions and entry qualifications demanded, institutions themselves are not equally attractive or accessible to all students. As summarised in the Ball report on access, 'from the point of view of the school leaver, qualified by A-levels, higher education may be seen as a nest of concentric circles, with highly selective universities like Oxford and Cambridge at the centre, surrounded first by the other universities, then by the polytechnics, then by the colleges of higher and further education. Mature students see things differently: for them the Open University, the polytechnics and further education colleges are most important' (Ball, 1989).

Our own previous work has pointed to the differing entry patterns into particular subjects and courses with a tendency for courses in the subject areas of arts/humanities and the social sciences to offer wider opportunities for entry to applicants without A-level qualifications. As mature entrants to higher education are less likely to possess A-levels, such students are also attracted to these subject areas (Brennan and McGeevor, 1988). There is also an institutional difference with respect to entry qualifications, and there are *science* subject areas which in polytechnics attract and accept students with fewer entry qualifications than equivalent courses in universities. The continuity of this trend, and the extent of the differences between individual subject areas, can be seen from our more recent survey.

A couple of important things stand out from Tables 3.2. and 3.3. First, there is the clustering of the university courses in the sample towards the higher end of the ranked tables. The ability both to demand and to receive candidates with higher A-level point scores is much stronger in the universities. The second important point to note is the extent of the difference between subject areas within polytechnics, with subjects such as law, estate management, business studies and modern languages being able to command considerably higher entry qualifications than courses such as general science, biology, social science and humanities. Whether this is so because of higher demand for places, enabling course teams to pick and choose amongst candidates, or because of different recruitment criteria being adopted in different subject areas cannot be assessed from the evidence presented here, but would require a closer look at the nature of admissions procedures – still very much 'the secret backyard' of higher education.

The extent to which A-level point scores constitute reliable measures of the academic quality of student entrants is open to question, as is the extent to which the possession of a degree can compensate in the labour market for lower standard secondary school qualifications. The 'value addedness' of an undergraduate or post-graduate degree relative to earlier educational credentials is a topic to which we shall return later. What is beyond doubt is that the *breadth* of educational experience students bring with them to higher education varies considerably between institutions and between subject areas,

**Table 3.2: Proportions of students with 6 or more
A-level points (1985 survey)**

Course	Proportion (%)
Biology	22.6
Social Sciences	23.8
Science	24.8
Mechanical Engineering	25.0
Quantity Surveying	28.2
Fine Art	28.8
3D Design	30.3
Textile/Fashion	31.3
Education	34.0
Humanities	34.0
Sport Recreation	35.6
Electrical Engineering	36.6
Graphic Design	38.8
Performing Arts	40.1
Architecture	40.6
Combined Studies	42.4
Computing	42.8
Economics	44.5
Business	46.3
Modern Languages	47.2
Accountancy	49.0
Communication Studies	59.7
Estate Management	60.3
Law	64.8
U Computing	70.5
U Mechanical Engineering	73.5
U History/English	87.2
U Biology	92.2
U Economics	94.6
U Accountancy	94.8

Table 3.3: Proportions of students with 9 or more A-level points (1985 survey)

Course	Proportion (%)
Science	6.0
Biology	6.1
Social Science	6.3
Sport Recreation	6.5
Humanities	6.7
Economics	7.8
Quantity Surveying	7.8
Mechanical Engineering	8.0
Fine Art	9.5
Education	10.0
Electrical Engineering	10.3
Accountancy	10.9
Performing Arts	11.0
Combined Studies	11.3
Computing	11.8
Textile/Fashion	13.0
Architecture	13.3
Graphic Design	14.3
Business	14.8
Modern Languages	15.9
3D Design	16.2
Law	18.6
Communication Studies	21.8
Estate Management	26.1
U Computing	47.3
U Mechanical Engineering	63.3
U History/English	73.3
U Biology	79.1
U History/En	82.3
U Accountancy	87.5
All	23.9

the consequences of which for labour market recruitment practices need further investigation.

Social Demand and Educational Choice

The relationship between the needs in the economy for skills and the demand in the population for higher education is tenuous. Individual determinants of educational choice play an important role in defining career orientations and the demand for higher education. The social demand for higher education is not only an issue of increasing participation rates as such, but also of understanding the structure of that demand relative to particular courses and subject areas. Parental background, community characteristics, family pressures, economic status, gender, all influence such individual determinants both as regards the decisions to enter higher education as such, as well as choice of which particular discipline or subject area to study. The career development process takes place over a long time, and educational choices constitute only intermediary stages in this process. They are stages, however, which may have fundamental consequences for future labour market opportunities. General economic incentives may guide the pursuit of higher education in general, in that most graduates are eventually rewarded with higher incomes than non-graduates. But also people study for reasons other than those of obtaining specific labour market skills and jobs. In the light of this, it becomes important to look at the heterogeneity of the student population and the various aims that students pursue in higher education.

Previous research, both under the auspices of the HELM Project and elsewhere, indicates that there are broadly two sets of educational goals, one concerned with providing qualifications so that a living can be earned, usually referred to as 'extrinsic' or 'pragmatic' goals; the other not directly tied to employment but concerned more generally with social and cultural self-development – 'intrinsic' goals. Evidence indicates that influences of the labour market and concern for financial rewards are important, but not in equal measure for all students in all subject areas. It is also the case that students do not formulate well-defined vocational preferences at the same point in their career. Some entrants to higher education already have well developed vocational aims, others wish to keep their options open longer. Such factors affect subject choice, and it is important to know how they are structured across the student population with consequent effects on the 'social catchment' of particular courses and subject areas.

Evidence from the 1982 HELM panel revealed that graduates from different courses show unanimity in what they regarded as the purpose of higher education, with the greatest importance overall being attached to 'the generation of new knowledge', followed by 'personal growth and the development of the individual' and 'the training of highly qualified specialists for industry and commerce'. Students sharing a common ideology about the main functions of higher education nevertheless differ in their personal aspirations about which of these functions they as individuals look for in their higher education experience. International comparative studies of higher education and the labour market also point to the desire among many students for a 'broad' approach to higher education that allows intrinsic as well as extrinsic values to be pursued. In a recent European study it was shown that in most countries, when presented with a choice between studying a subject they find interesting or one offering good future career prospects, most students opted for the former possibility (Dippelhofer-Stien, 1984; Sanyal, 1987). Research in France shows that when the career aspects of courses can be combined with more intrinsic cultural aspects, the demand for such courses increases. All studies seem to agree, however, that whichever way orientations are looked at, students in some subject areas show a greater propensity for extrinsic, pragmatic and materialistic values than in others, and that this is so despite a shared and general understanding of the relative financial positions of various occupational groups in the labour market.

The HELM data allows us to explore the notion of 'student orientation' a bit further in order to isolate clusters of factors that enter into motivations and choice in higher education, and to relate such clusters both to the chosen subject of study. The Wave One questionnaire administered to the 1982 graduate panel two years after graduation (see Chapter Two) asked a range of questions directed at the occupational orientations and self-perceptions of students in particular subject areas. Graduates were asked to indicate the importance of a series of items to their choice of a long-term job, and to mark the importance of various spheres of life to them, as well as to give an indication of how they thought of themselves. Factor analysis of these sets of questions allows the isolation of four orientation types: 'careerist'; 'inner-directed work'; 'altruistic'; and 'leisure'.

The 'careerist' orientation correlates strongly with:

'strong possibility of rapid promotion' (.76);
'high prestige and social status' (.69);
'high salary' (.67);
'considerable job security' (.57);

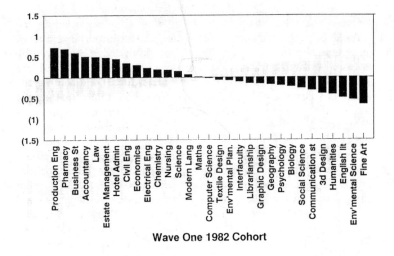

Figure 3.4: Job orientation type 'careerist'

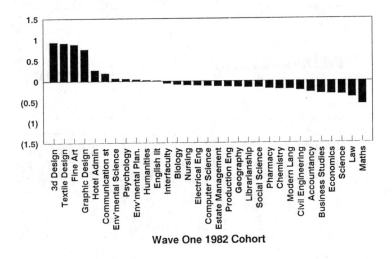

Figure 3.5: Job orientation type 'inner directed worker'

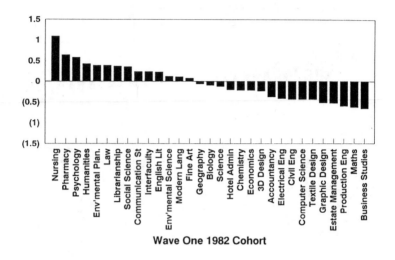

Figure 3.6: Job orientation type 'altruistic orientation'

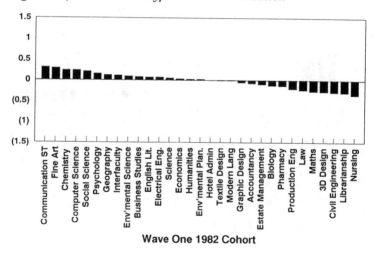

Figure 3.7: Job orientation type 'leisure orientation'

'opportunity for professional development' (.56);
'the chance to exercise leadership' (.56).

Looking at Figure 3.4. we see that the most 'careerist' courses are of a vocational kind and include production engineering, pharmacy, business studies and accountancy. The least careerist are fine art, environmental science, English literature and the humanities. The scale in Figures 3.4, 3.5, 3.6 and 3.7 is in terms of standard deviation. Thus, production engineering graduates score an average .73 above the sample mean. Fine art graduates score .66 below the mean (with 95% of the sample scoring between +1.96 and -1.96 of the mean).

The 'inner-directed work' orientation is strongly related to the following:

'the opportunity to be creative' (.72);
'opportunity to use one's special skills and abilities' (.69)
'relative freedom from supervision from others' (.64)
'work that is continually challenging' (.60).

As this is almost by definition the orientation of the artist, it is perhaps not surprising to find the art and design courses occupying the first four places. Courses in hotel and catering also score highly on this. At the other extreme are graduates in maths, law, science and economics, who are more concerned about financial rewards (see Figure 3.5.).

The 'altruistic' orientation is characterised by a wish to devote one's life and work to others, and correlates highly with the following:

'opportunity to help others' (.88)
'potential for improving society' (.71)
'opportunity to work with people' (.71)

The subject areas where courses include the greatest proportion of 'altruistically' orientated students are nursing, pharmacy, psychology and humanities. Those showing least 'altruism' are business studies, maths, production engineering and urban estate management (Figure 3.6.).

The last job orientation type is that of a 'leisure orientation', which is constituted by the following:

'considerable leisure time' (.69);
'flexible working hours' (.59);
'work which is not too exacting' (.59).

It should be noted here that the range of values is smaller than in the other factors, and that differences were not usually large. This means that there are a few graduates on most courses who have this orientation. It does not characterise a particular subject area. That students on professional courses such as nurses, civil engineers and librarians are the least leisure-orientated could perhaps be expected. At the other end, communications and fine arts students are more leisure-oriented, as are applied chemistry and computer science students. There may be some jobs which are seen as suitable for earning money quickly and independently, thus leaving time for the pursuit of more central values.

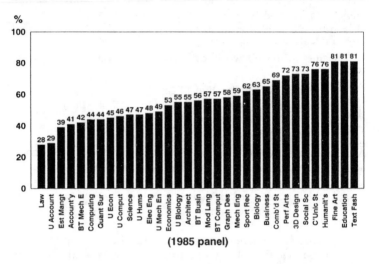

Figure 3.8: Reasons for doing further study: personal interest

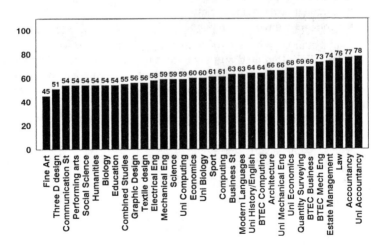

Figure 3.9: Reason for doing further study: career prospects

Subject differences in the career orientations of students are also seen when we look at the reasons graduates give for entering further study, with again some courses characterised by motivations related to careers and other characterised by personal interests (Figures 3.8. and 3.9.).

Attempts within the labour market to regulate demand by increasing wages to attract recruits will only influence student choice of courses so long as the students regard immediate financial rewards as their main guiding principle. We have seen that not everyone does. Students with a 'careerist' orientation are most likely to be sensitive to 'cues' from the 'altruistically' motivated students or 'inner-directed' students. The latter are also concerned about work, but may well respond more slowly to labour market fluctuations in demand, conditions and pay. The 'careerist' orientation (with its emphasis on the extrinsic rewards of higher education), characteristic of students in the subject areas discussed above, is not unrelated either to the educational status of such courses relative to entry standards nor to the gender, age and social composition of those courses.

Women students, mature students and students from a lower class background express more of an 'altruistic', 'inner-directed' than a 'careerist' orientation (Figures 3.10., 3.11. 3.12.).

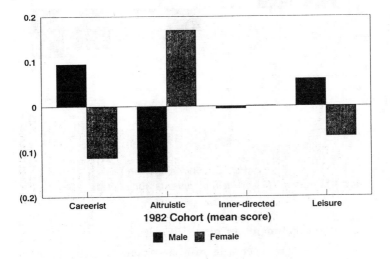

Figure 3.10: Job orientation by gender: male and female score

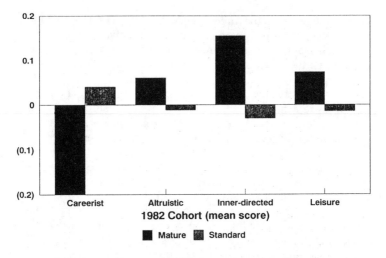

Figure 3.11: *Job orientation by age: mature and standard entrant score*

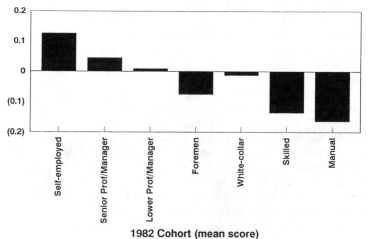

1982 Cohort (mean score)
Figure 3.12: *'Careerist orientation': parents' social class*

The Social Catchment of Course Recruitment

With a declining number of 18-year-olds entering higher education, admission trends already well established over the last 20 years will continue. The participation of women will continue to increase, as will that of mature students in general. Some courses traditionally recruiting mainly middle-class young people will have to widen their catchment, as will employers in search of graduate labour power. It is beyond the confines of this book to give a detailed description of the 'social catchment' of individual subject areas and course types. Given the institutional differences pointed to above, and differences between the aims and objectives of individual courses, it is also likely that there are differences between individual courses in the type of student they attract.

The most important background characteristic of students influencing both student orientations and choice of course, which is also of direct relevance to labour market recruitment practices, is that of gender. There is ample evidence that women approach education with different aims and interests from those of men, and consequently tend to choose different subjects. The persistent gender 'divide' between the technological and the human sciences, the private and the public sector, and full-time and part-time work are well documented (Acker and Warren Piper, 1984; IMS 1990; Redpath and Harvey, 1987; Thomas, 1990). Women are less guided by financial and status rewards in their approach to education than men, and financial market mechanisms may not be enough to redirect their choices to more technologically and financially orientated subjects. The differences in subject choice away from numerically based subjects appear early, as can be seen from Table 3.13., which shows the educational background of the women on the wide range of courses surveyed among the 1982 panel.

This means that for women students, options of studying in the subject areas of technology, science and also business and finance related subjects soon become closed. Table 3.14. shows the gender distribution of students in a large number of subject areas among the 1982 panel of graduates. The same distribution can be seen in the 1985 panel. Research on the aspirations of school leavers in general strongly reinforces the impression that women see the value of higher education in more 'intrinsic' terms and tend to opt for subjects both in school and in higher education that are 'people-orientated' and in our earlier terminology 'altruistic', rather than leading to better pay and faster career advancement (Redpath and Harvey, 1987). There is an ongoing interaction between gender, motivations, career orientations and choice of study, the effects of which carry over into the labour market. These are long-term, well-established cultural patterns which are not easy to shift.

Students, Courses and Jobs

**Table 3.13: GCE and CSE examination passes by gender
(1982 HELM panel)**

	Men	Women	- N -
Home Management	---	100.0	10**
D.S. (Cookery)	4.1	95.9	196***
Secretarial Studies	4.2	95.8	24***
D.S. (Needlework)	7.6	92.4	92***
Typewriting	15.4	84.6	39***
Psychology	30.4	69.6	23*
Music	34.5	65.5	110***
Sociology	34.9	65.1	189***
German	35.5	64.5	358***
Human Biology	35.6	64.4	174***
Drama/Human Movement	36.4	63.6	22
European Studies	36.4	63.6	11
Latin or Greek	36.6	63.4	284***
Classical Studies	37.5	62.5	32*
French	40.9	59.1	1315***
Other Language	40.9	59.1	164***
Art & Craft	43.1	56.9	727***
Economic History	43.9	56.1	41
Biology	44.1	55.9	1271***
English Literature	45.4	54.6	1811***
Religious Studies	45.7	54.3	346**
Commerce	46.3	53.7	82
History	48.2	51.8	1252***
Other Science	49.6	50.4	133
Social Studies	51.1	48.9	45
English Language	52.3	46.8	2259
Humanities	53.8	46.2	13
Welsh or Gaelic	54.2	45.8	24
Arithmetic	54.5	45.5	235
English Oral	54.7	45.3	53
Geography	54.8	45.2	1415*
General Studies	54.8	45.2	546
Mathematics	55.2	44.8	2077***
Local/Rural Studies	56.1	43.9	41
Chemistry	62.6	37.4	1099***

Table 3.13: GCE and CSE examination passes by gender
(1982 HELM panel) (continued)

General Science	63.8	36.2	69*
Geology	65.2	34.8	138**
Accountancy	65.9	34.1	85*
Economics	66.9	33.1	450***
British Government	67.1	32.9	149***
Computer Studies	69.6	30.4	56*
Additional Maths	69.6	30.4	369***
Design & Ceramics	73.7	26.3	19*
Physics	73.7	26.3	1144***
Woodwork	91.7	8.3	84***
Technical Drawing	95.4	4.6	284***
Metalwork	97.6	2.4	83***
Applied Mechanics	100.0	---	18***
Percent Male/Female	52.9	47.1	2660

+ Excluding subjects studied by fewer than ten respondents
*** $p<0.001$ ** $p<0.01$* $p<0.1$
Source: Gatley, 1988

A second student characteristic of labour market relevance is that of age. From Table 3.15. we can see the extent of age differentiation between courses in the subject areas chosen by the 1985 panel, which provides further evidence to that presented in the previous HELM graduate survey report. While earlier findings point to the academic success of mature students (age 21 or over at entry to higher education), subsequent entry to the labour market may be affected by the institution attended, career orientation and consequent choice of subject and course. The university courses in the 1985 panel have a smaller proportion of mature students than polytechnic courses in the same subject areas. Polytechnic courses in the areas of social sciences and humanities have by far the largest proportions of mature students. In the case of social science it is close to half. These are also courses, as we have shown, characterised by the lack of strong 'career orientations', as here defined, on the part of their students. There are also a few polytechnic engineering subjects with sizeable proportions of mature students.

Table 3.14: Subjects undertaken by graduate men
and women (1982 HELM panel)

	Men %	Women %	Number
Nursing	6.2	93.8	65
Textiles	11.5	88.5	87
Modern Languages	20.0	80.0	85
English Literature	23.6	76.4	55
Librarianship	27.0	73.0	100
Psychology	27.7	72.3	83
Hotel Administration	27.8	72.2	72
Interfaculty	37.7	62.3	151
Humanities	39.9	60.1	163
Communication Studies	42.7	57.3	96
Fine Art	43.1	56.9	72
Social Studies	46.7	53.3	122
Three D Design	50.6	49.4	83
Graphic Design	51.6	48.4	95
Science	58.7	41.3	143
Geography	60.7	39.3	89
Law	61.4	38.6	57
Pharmacy	61.7	38.3	81
Applied Biology	62.2	37.8	135
Environmental Science	64.7	35.3	85
Mathematics	64.8	35.2	54
Computer Science	66.7	33.3	54
Business Studies	67.6	32.4	105
Accountancy	73.1	26.9	53
Economics	77.8	22.2	54
Environmental Planning	82.5	17.5	63
Applied Chemistry	83.6	16.4	73
Urban Estate Management	86.6	13.4	82
Mech & Elec Engineering	98.1	1.9	53
Civil Engineering	98.5	1.5	66
Production Engineering	100.0	----	55
All	53.1	46.9	2630

**Table 3.15: Percentage of mature students at entry
by course (1985 panel)**

U Biology	.0
BT Business Studies	2.9
U Accounting	3.2
Biology	4.0
Accountancy	4.6
U Economics	4.7
BT Mechanical Engineering	5.6
U History EN	6.4
U Computing	6.4
Textile Fashion	6.5
U Mechanical EN	6.9
Computing	8.8
Science	9.0
BT Computer	10.5
Sport & Recreation	11.2
Estate Management	11.3
3D Design	12.2
Modern Language	12.5
Economics	12.9
Business	13.2
Electrical Engineering	13.7
Architecture	15.2
Graphic Design	15.5
Fine Art	17.1
Communication Studies	17.3
Mechanical Engineering	19.5
Performance Arts	20.2
Combined Studies	21.6
Law	22.4
Quantity Surveying	23.5
Education	28.0
Humanities	31.0
Social Science	41.6
All	**12.9**

Finally, it is worth looking at the relationship between subject choice and social class, crudely measured by father's occupation and type of secondary school attended (Figures 3.16. and 3.17.). University courses appear in the top half of both charts, as do professional courses such as accountancy, estate management, architecture and business studies. Polytechnic social science and engineering courses appear at the lower end. Traditionally, working-class men and

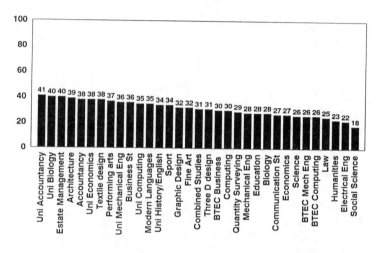

Figure 3.16: Proportion of fathers in senior professional and managerial jobs (1985 panel)

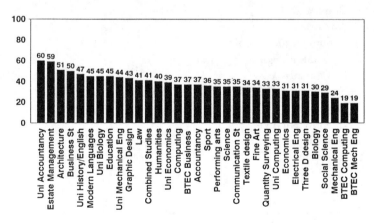

Figure 3.17: Proportions who attended grammar and fee paying schools (1985 panel)

women and mature students have seen such subject areas and courses in polytechnics as avenues for upward mobility. Whether and how to channel these students into other subjects and skills areas will be one of the challenges for higher education in the next decade.

Conclusion

In a free market of places in higher education, the matching of the complex pattern of social demand with labour market needs is unlikely to become much closer without some transformation of both student orientations and employer flexibility in improving the conditions for fulfilment of aims other than career advancement and financial success. Questions also arise for the structure of courses and qualifications. Early specialisation blocks off options later on. By international standards, the short and specialist nature of the English honours degree forces upon students choices which may be undesirable and unnecessary. Many students will be both 'careerist' and 'inner directed'. Are there sufficient opportunities currently available within higher education which allow them to be both?

The flow of students into courses will depend on decisions made by students, and by higher education institutions within the financial structures set for them. The marketing of courses and jobs will, in the light of the above, have to direct itself to a heterogenous group of people with very different demands and expectations of both higher education and the labour market. It is to the nature of the latter that we will now turn.

A Segmented Labour Market

Introduction and Summary

Guided by the analytical model of the 'helm' relationship developed in the previous chapter, Chapter Four focuses on one of the two markets mediated by higher education courses. It will outline the features of and trends in the graduate labour market with reference to the interplay between the supply of and the demand for graduates; the factors and considerations which impinge upon employer demand and thereby graduate recruitment and opportunities; the relevance and importance of graduate labour market variety and segmentation; and the implications with regard to higher education policy and course design and recruitment. At the same time, the chapter examines the graduate labour market by emphasising the relevance of student 'social catchment' and orientations.

The 1980s saw a shift in the occupational structure in favour of 'knowledge based' labour, skills and 'competences', and therefore in favour of graduate employment. The resulting improvement in the graduate labour market, demand and opportunities was accompanied by an associated expansion of higher education institutions, places and students. At the same time, however, the prevailing demographic patterns and trends (touched on in previous chapters) brought a sizeable reduction in the availability for higher education courses, and thereby the graduate labour market, of 'traditional' younger ('school leaver') candidates. In turn, this particular development has been accompanied by a somewhat countervailing increase in the numbers and proportions of older candidates – and more especially of older female candidates – which has then fed into the graduate labour market.

There is the persistence of a strong relationship between gender and a labour market that is both horizontally segmented and vertically hierarchical: a pattern which applies just as much to the graduate labour market as to any other portion. In other words, despite changes favouring the greater participation of women in the graduate labour market linked to higher education, there is plenty of evidence which indicates the resilience of a 'dual labour market' differentiating men and women, whereby each continue to gravitate and be pulled towards a certain range of graduate jobs. In sum, there remains a graduate labour market which is clearly and firmly both segmented and hierarchical along gender lines (Lyon and Murray, forthcoming).

The chapter assesses the implications of the links between the segmented graduate labour market and higher education for participants in this market (employers and graduates); for student preparation for the graduate labour market; for course development, design and designers; for course recruitment; for higher education course candidates; and for those involved in social and educational policy formulation and implementation.

Employment Trends in the 1980s and 1990s

In an employer-based study of employment trends in the 1980s, the Institute of Manpower Studies presented a picture of changes in sectorial distribution within the UK occupational structure, some of which have a direct bearing on changing employment trends for graduates during the period surveyed, as well as into the 1990s. In 1985, employment within production industries and agriculture constituted a third of the work force, with the remaining two thirds made up of service industries. Within the latter, the largest sector is made up of distributive, financial and business services, and amongst production industries, engineering and related industries constitute the largest sector. Overall, production industries were expected to reduce their workforce overall by 8 per cent, and the service industries were expected to increase by 3.6 per cent, especially within distributive, financial, business and leisure services. Whereas public sector employment was expected to fall, small firms and self-employment, as well as part-time employment, in general were expected to increase. Further, women's share in the work force was seen to continue to increase with the majority of new jobs expected to be filled by female, often part-time employees. However, within these overall changes in labour market trends, new technologies and organisational changes will continue to create a growth in skills and knowledge intensive areas, especially for technologists, engineers and scientists, as well as in the area of management and management support services such as accountants, data processors, marketing specialists and so forth. Sectorial changes will mean a shift towards occupations with higher knowledge content, and will on the whole create more favourable employment conditions for particular kinds of graduates than for other less qualified potential employees (Pearson and Rajan, 1986).

Since 1979, the public sector share of the total work force in employment has continued to fall both on a head count, and on the basis of full-time equivalents. Between 1982 and 1988 it fell from 29.4 per cent to 24.5 per cent, with more women than men working in part-time occupations. The NHS and education account for 51 per cent of all public sector employees. A significant proportion of this fall stems from privatisation of public corporations. This decline in the public sector could be anticipated to have a direct effect on the employability of graduates from courses traditionally serving the public sector, such as courses in the Humanities, and we need to see whether there has been a change during the 1980s towards employment in the private sector for graduates in these subjects. The trend towards the reduction of the public sector looks like continuing into the 1990s (Fleming, 1988).

With government support, self-employment is a growing phenomenon within the British economy. Between 1981 and 1984 self-employment grew by approximately 20 per cent. In the labour market as a whole, in 1984 11.2 per cent of all employed persons were self-employed. It is on the whole a male phenomenon, with three quarters of all self-employed persons being men. Given the skills, capital and experience needed to get established in self-employment, it is also more prevalent amongst the middle-aged, with only 17 per cent being under 30 years of age. There is a dominance in particular industries especially distribution, hotel and catering, construction and other services, and in the managerial categories. Despite self-employment being a growing form of economic activity in Britain, the UK has a lower population of self-employment than many other EC countries. Some polytechnic courses are beginning to approach the issues facing those in search of self-employment, for example Textiles and Design courses. Given the government policy of fostering a general attitude of individual enterprise and a policy towards encouraging self-employment, it is important for the HELM project to look into course and subject areas where students attempt to set up and develop their own enterprises. There has also been a growth in the number of small firms, including those seeking to recruit graduates (Craigh *et al.* 1986).

These overall changes in employment trends are taking place within a shifting age structure of the working population as a whole. This also has a direct bearing on graduate employment prospects. There is a predicted continued rise overall in the size of the labour force (people aged 16 or over in paid employment or seeking work) with most of the projected rise to occur in the female labour force because of a continued rise in activity rates. The proportion of women in the labour force as a whole rose from 37 per cent in 1971 to 44 per cent in 1987, and is expected to rise further in the next decade. (The proportion of women in higher education rose from 29 per cent in 1965–66 to 41 per cent of the student population in 1985–86.) This rise is offset by the fall of under 25-year-olds in the labour force from 23 per cent in 1987 to 18 per cent in 1985. Overall, the acute unemployment problems of the late 1970s and early 1980s for both graduates and other employees could be attributed partly to the high rate of increase in the population of working age in the late 1970s and early 1980s, due to a combination of high level of 'entries' and low level of 'exits'. This demographic change is expected to affect in a positive direction the employment prospects in particular sectors of the graduate labour market, and to raise real problems concerning the ability of higher education to fill the labour market demand in some growing areas of the economy. The role of women in the labour market can be expected to be more central to meeting labour market needs. With education still segmented according to gender in many significant ways, there is a need for greater attention to be paid to the progress of women through school into higher education and later into the labour market (Employment Gazette, March 1988 and April 1989, Pearson and Pike, 1989).

The Graduate Labour Market in the 1980s and Beyond

Graduates constitute only a small, though a growing part of the working population as a whole, (6% in 1987), and 11 per cent of all graduates in the labour market are under 24 years old. Yet graduates, both old and new, form a very significant part of the growth in managerial, technological, financial and other professional sectors of the economy, and employment prospects for graduates have been better over the last decade than for other groups despite the fact that the years between 1975 and 1985 witnessed a dramatic growth in the number of graduates entering the labour market, with a rise of 26 per cent for university graduates and 154 per cent for polytechnic graduates. Graduate employment is highly concentrated with over half of graduate employees in the 'other services' sector of industry and a further 18 per cent in 'banking, finance and insurance' in 1987. Almost 90 per cent is found in the 'managerial and professional' occupational group. The industries where employment grew during the 1980s were on the whole industries where the demand for graduates has been strong, such as professional services (covering accountancy, banking and insurance), other private services (covering retailing, hotels and catering) and health and welfare professions. 25.7 per cent of total graduate employment (37.5 per cent of female graduate

Students, Courses and Jobs

employment) is in education. Part-time employment and self-employment rose more rapidly than full-time employment, especially for women (33% and 71% respectively between 1983 and 1987), although graduates continue to be under-represented in small industries. Unemployment has fallen since 1983 and is relatively low (3.8% for males and 5.7% for females in 1987). Overall labour force participation for graduates is significantly above that for the population as a whole (Creigh and Rees, 1989).

Tarsh has for several years provided a general picture of changing trends in graduate employment patterns, using Early Destination Statistics. This has been supplemented by Meadows and Cox, who rely for some of their conclusions on evidence from the Institute for Employment Research (Meadows and Cox, 1987; Tarsh, 1985 and 1986). Persistent over time have been variations in employment patterns related to degree subject, as well as in relation to gender, institution and degree class. These differences between subjects cut across arts/science boundaries, so that, for instance, some science subjects have shown similar profiles to arts subjects. Subjects with above average employment rates shortly after graduation have been in the main engineering subjects, maths/computing, physics, and business related social sciences such as business studies and accountancy. These subject differences have been shown to persist despite the fact that, according to AGCAS, some 40 per cent of the current vacancies for new graduates are available to people with degrees in any subjects, and their persistence has become part of the policy debate in higher education. As pointed out by Meadows and Cox, graduates who are only eligible for vacancies open to graduates of any discipline have a far more limited choice of jobs than those also suitable for vacancies in a specific discipline.

The biggest increase in the numbers of both university and polytechnic graduates entering employment has been in the service sector, of distributive, business and leisure services, excluding public services and transport. Even in the difficult years between 1980 and 1985, the growth rate in this sector was 9 per cent a year. This sector has also been shown to recruit graduates from a wide range of disciplines. As has been discussed above, it is also a sector expected to continue to grow. A further growth area has been that of professional, mainly financial services, which has led to some professions such as accountancy becoming almost entirely graduate occupations. The annual growth in this sector between 1980 and 1984 was 3 per cent. 1985 saw an even further growth in this sector of nearly 14 per cent over the 1984 level. This sector recruits from all subjects, but 40 per cent of the recruits come from the disciplines of maths, business and management studies, economics and accountancy. There has been a decline in the proportion of arts graduates going into this sector. The engineering sector has also seen a growth in the demand for graduates, especially for general or combined engineering graduates with maths and computer skills. This demand is likely to continue to grow. This raises some concern in view of the imminent shortage of school leaver entrants to higher education and the fact that any potential growth in the graduate labour force as a whole is expected to come from the increasing activity rate of women, not a group traditionally associated with engineering and technological subjects or with careers in these areas.

In line with general sectorial changes in the economy, there has been a fall in the proportion of graduates recruited into varieties of public administration, from a third to a fifth of all graduates and the situation in this sector is likely to remain static. This is an area of recruitment which traditionally has shown a demand for both generalist and specialist graduates. Further areas of the graduate labour market where there has been little if any growth over the decade have been construction, public utilities, other manufacturing and education. With the decline in the school population, the demand for teachers fell sharply. This has had an effect right across the board for graduates, but especially for those coming from arts and humanities disciplines. (Since the mid-1970s the proportion of university and polytechnic graduates entering teacher training has approximately halved.) The very recent growth in the demand for teachers may change this situation, though given the tightening structure of a new core curriculum, may not profit all subjects in higher education equally.

Looking towards the future, existing evidence suggests that growth occupations will be managers, administrators, engineers, scientists and technologists, research and development orientated staff and the professions in general. This will continue to mean a shift in demand away from arts and humanities graduates, and those with general non-numerate education towards graduates in more numerate, managerial and technological subjects, that is, some graduates will continue to face some difficulties in the labour market, whilst there will be a continuing shortage of others. Sectorial differences within the graduate labour market will continue with a process of 'filtering down' in the labour market continuing for some graduates in less demand, for example into administrative and secretarial work, whereas other occupational areas will continue to display signs of changing into graduate domains, especially those general service areas where the introduction of new technologies is increasing skill contents, and areas of product marketing and of management in general (Meadows and Cox, 1987; Wilson *et al.* 1990).

With declining cohorts of 18-year-olds entering higher education, there is a great deal of concern expressed about how the demand for graduate labour in some sectors of the economy is to be filled. Pearson refers to this problem as 'a time bomb in the making'. This demand can only be filled either by a shift of student entry from some subjects into others, or by the growing number of mature students entering higher education. A growing focus on mature students by both employers and the government has also meant a special stress on the role of women in the labour market, since this is a category for which activity rates in the labour market are increasing and likely to continue to increase for some time. Recent analysis of the FDS, however, has led to concern being expressed over the employment prospects of mature graduates. FDS for UK graduates in 1983 and 1984 indicated that fewer mature graduates found themselves in employment and more in the 'other' destination categories (Phillips, 1987). Largest differences were found in the 'not available for employment' category, where mature women especially showed higher rates than conventional age females and males (approximately 8% over both years). It is suggested that higher education as a whole has a more flexible approach to work schedules and child care than do employers, and hence is more able to attract and retain women.

For our present purposes, however, the important finding from this analysis is that the labour market status of mature students varies according to subject area. In education and agriculture, the mature graduates were shown to fare better in getting jobs than younger graduates; in engineering there was no difference shown, but in the areas of sciences, administrative and business studies, languages and art, the mature graduate fared worse than the conventional age graduate. Furthermore, mature graduates were more likely to be faced with temporary jobs. In view of some of the labour market difficulties of mature graduates, and of the need for the economy to recruit more mature people, especially women, it will be important to look at the distribution of mature students across degree subjects, as well as at their employment progress and factors, such as family responsibilities, that might provide a hindrance. The pressure on higher education establishments to recruit more mature, non-standard graduates, especially into the areas of science, engineering and information technology, is likely to increase. Whether they will succeed or not may depend upon why particular students choose to study particular subjects (Phillips, 1987; Tarsh, 1989).

Towards the end of the 1980s, the graduate labour market appeared a more buoyant place to enter for some, though by no means all graduates, than it did ten years earlier. Yet by 1991, the picture had deteriorated sharply again. For employers it will gradually become

a more difficult market within which to fill their growing demands
for particular skills.

Students into Employment: a Process of Segmentation

There are several conclusions and implications arising from the
discussion in this chapter.

1. During the last few years, a great deal of detailed research has
   been undertaken on the relationship between the nature of
   the course undertaken by a student and entry into the
   labour market. This research has shown a strong
   relationship between subjects and early employment status
   using several indicators such as speed of entry, income, level
   of work, quality of work and so on. Models for the nature of
   this relationship have been developed indicating how
   different types of courses relate to different labour market
   conditions for students. There appears to be no demand in
   the labour market for graduates as such, only for particular
   types of graduates in particular markets more or less
   regulated. The evidence indicates the need to get away from
   a uni-dimensional model of both 'graduate' and 'the
   graduate labour market' (Brennan and McGeevor, 1988;
   Boys and Kirkland, 1988).

2. By the time students come to choose a course of study, they
   have already been the subjects of a lengthy process of
   educational differentiation partly as a result of the effects of
   characteristics such as gender, class, and ethnicity. The
   choice of a higher education course is in itself an outcome of
   a process that can be termed 'pre-labour market
   segmentation'. As the labour market for graduates is in itself
   segmented both vertically, into more or less secure and well
   paid jobs, and horizontally, between job sectors more or less
   'closed' to only those graduates with particular types of
   skills and combinations of qualifications, the task of
   'matching' student backgrounds, aspirations and skills with
   particular labour markets lies at the heart of the role of
   degree courses in the labour market.

3. Courses can be seen to matter to employers in the way they
   convey information about graduates mainly on two counts:
   about the types of skills a graduate can be expected to
   possess, and about the nature of his or her motivations and
   orientations towards particular types of work. As different
   types of employers operate within different, and over time

changing, segments of the labour market, graduates can not
be aggregated in a simple fashion to indicate met or unmet
demand in various sectors. Producing 'more' or 'less'
graduates is not itself a solution to the various problems of
'mismatch', nor is immediate responsiveness in terms of
increased 'vocationalism' in higher education in general
going to solve problems that arise from skills shortages in
earlier stages of the educational system, or seen to be
determined by extra educational motivational factors related
for example to gender and age.

Previous work on the HELM graduate panel survey for 1982 graduates showed the extent of course differences in outcomes over time
on several indicators, and laid the ground work for more theoretical
work on the different types of relationship courses may have with
sectors of the labour market. It also, along with other surveys, pointed
towards the differences in the nature of the intake of students on
different courses. Though almost all graduates were in employment
three years on, it was still apparent that different courses exhibited
different trajectories of entry into different types of labour market
conditions. Markets change over time, however, both in employer
demand and in the types of sectors in growth or decline. So do student
aspirations and choices. It is one of the aims of the present report to
approach these questions longitudinally, by looking in greater detail
at entry trajectories of two cohort panels, 1982 and 1985, for the first
three years after graduation. Are the trajectories the same? Are the
improvements in some sectors on the labour market reflected in all?
Are the gender factors affecting choice of courses constant over time,
along with labour market status, or has there been a shift in the
market? Given the significance of pre-segmentation, particularly
through differential admissions policies of courses, more attention
will also be paid to changing student experiences in the labour market
relative to previous student qualifications and other relevant characteristics such as age, gender, ethnicity and social class.

Chapter Five

The Changing Graduate Labour Market

Introduction and Summary

This chapter carries forward the theme of Chapter Four by continuing to focus on the graduate labour market. It is concerned with graduate labour market change and its implications for the 'helm' relationship; more specifically, it examines graduate labour market fluctuations during the 1980s into the 1990s, especially with reference to their consequences for higher education students, course and subjects. The chapter explores the possibility that recent graduate labour market developments have been more important for certain students, courses and subjects than for others. It does so by comparing the experiences of the 1982 and 1985 graduate panels.

Various sources of evidence outside the HELM project – such as the First Destinations Statistics (FDS) – firmly show that there have been sizeable fluctuations in graduate labour market conditions and employment prospects during the 1980s. Most notably there was a considerable improvement over the decade in the rate and speed of graduate employment take-up *relative to non-graduates*. In effect, even though there was an expansion in the number of higher education students leading to an increase on the supply side of the graduate labour market, there was what amounts to more than compensatory increase on the demand side. There was enhanced buoyancy in the graduate labour market reflecting major shifts in employer demands and occupational requirements linked to underlying economic developments.

The HELM project data confirms how the 1985 national cohort of graduates enjoyed what appear to be a more favourable labour market than the 1982 cohort, while both (a) highlighting the complex features of the patterns and trends involved; and (b) inviting caution against any simplistic explanatory interpretation of the patterns and trends. While the data shows that the 1985 cohort entered employment more fully and quickly than the 1982 cohort, it also suggests that this trend reflects something other than more and better graduate labour market demand, conditions and opportunities.

The chapter raises the possibility that student/graduate perceptions about the labour market – and in particular about options and opportunities with regard to employment and careers – play a crucial part in influencing patterns and trends in graduate employment take up, especially early on. Thus, the possibility arises of the greater and faster employment rate among 1985 graduates being to some extent a reflection of an enhanced sense of threat and fear of unemployment, making them somewhat less choosy and discriminatory over their employment take up. Graduate perceptions and fears with regard to labour market options and opportunities will help to explain the notable increase between the 1982 and 1985 cohorts in the proportions still in full-time education which, in turn, has fed into the reduction in the rate of graduate unemployment.

Moreover, just as Chapter Three emphasises how student orientations *vis-à-vis* higher education courses linked to employment are gender dependent, this chapter confirms how the 1980s' graduate labour market improvements were somewhat gender biased due in part to the way in which (a) women are inclined towards certain higher education subjects and courses rather than others; and (b) men are inclined to those higher education subjects and courses which have been differentially favoured by the complexities of the improvements. This is not to ignore the further point that, independent of variations in course/career orientations between men and women, there are further gender discriminations within the graduate labour market whereby men are simply more able to take advantage of the recent graduate labour market patterns and trends in demand, options and opportunities. It is not to ignore, in other words, the operation of a dual labour market along gender lines with integral and attendant inequalities of condition and opportunity in favour of men.

Given the links between (a) subjects/courses, (b) subject/course vocational associations and (c) gender, the chapter addresses the issue of the relative weighting to be given in an analysis of recent graduate labour market patterns and trends to (a) 'subject/course type' and (b) 'gender' as far as their influence on the extent, speed and type of employment take up is concerned.

The 1985 graduates appear to have entered a more buoyant labour market in that they entered with greater speed than the 1982 cohort. Either 1982 was a worse year, so that it took longer for the graduates to find employment, or 1985 was perceived by graduates to be a bad year in light of the experiences of graduates earlier in the decade, so that the 1985 graduates took the first job that came their way. The latter interpretation would explain not only the quick entry into the labour market and the continuing rates of high unemployment for some graduates but also the high rates of graduates in full-time study for the 1985 cohort in comparison with the 1982 cohort. With this interpretation in mind, the chapter will look at graduates' aspirations and career satisfactions. How does the speed of entry differ between the two cohorts and different subjects? Did the 1982 graduates feel they could take their time in deciding where and for whom they wanted to work? Did the 1985 graduates feel so insecure that they found a job quickly just to avoid being unemployed? If the 1985 graduates did take the first job that came along, they are probably more likely to feel overqualified for the jobs they are doing two years into the labour market. This will be discussed in relation to subject areas and the gender of graduates. The chapter will conclude that year of graduation does effect the relationship between degree subject and labour market outcomes, but does so unevenly between subject areas and between men and women.

Critical Discussion of Graduate Destinations

The First Destinations Statistics suggest that 1982 was a particularly bad year for graduates entering the labour market for the first time. The proportion of graduates from 1981 known to be still looking for work at the end of the year was 15 per cent. A further 15 per cent were 'unknowns'. Some 'still seeking' may have found employment or training courses over the early months of 1982, but as Scott (1982) suggests, there was a sizeable carry over of the previous year's graduates competing for jobs with the 1982 graduates. The search for employment, therefore, proved to take longer than in any previous year and affected some subjects more than others, as the HELM data have previously shown (Brennan and McGeevor, 1988).

For the 1985 cohort, according to the FDS data, the picture is somewhat brighter. Meadows and Cox (1987) using evidence from the University of Warwick Institute of Employment Research and the FDS show that between 1975 and 1984 (when the 1982 cohort were seeking employment) total UK employment fell by nearly 1.1 million (over 4%). Employment rose again by 250,000 between 1984 and 1985, when the 1985 graduates were seeking employment. This shows the different labour market conditions that the two cohorts were facing upon graduation.

A recent study of a large sample of employers examined their approach to graduate recruitment and their expectations for the early 1990s (DES 1990). The resulting report shows that the total number of graduates in the population will continue to grow rapidly as a result of the steady expansion of higher education since the 1960s, and that the number of students in higher education is at record levels. The report predicts that the demand for new graduates will continue to grow into the 1990s.

The DES output projections from 1989 to the year 2000 indicate that student numbers will grow rapidly into the early 1990s and that the effect of the 18 to 19 years age range reaching a low in the mid-1990s will be a flattening out of student numbers rather than a significant fall. Therefore, state the DES, there will not be a shortage of graduates in the labour market in the 1990s.

Along with this data, the Occupational Studies Group (OSG) forecasts suggest that there will be a shift in the occupational structure in the economy. The favoured occupations will be managers, administrators, engineers, scientists, technologists, research and design-related staff and the professions. These are the types of employment that graduates tend to enter. On the basis of this information, Meadows and Cox (1987) come to the conclusion that graduates in the 1990s should not experience any difficulty in gaining employment.

However, this prospect is highly conditional upon the subject of study undertaken. The subject studied bears a direct relationship to the type of labour market employment (Brennan and McGeevor, 1988; Meadows and Cox, 1987). Graduates in those subject areas that are in demand by employers will continue to have relatively low rates of unemployment in the 1990s while those subjects that tend to have relatively high rates of unemployment are likely to face fairly static, and in some cases falling, demand from employers.

From the above we can see that the demand for graduates is likely to continue to grow over the next few years, although the growth rates will not be uniform across subject areas. Graduates will not have equal labour market opportunities available to them because of the degree subject effect (albeit linked to social characteristics, such as ethnicity, age or gender).

Degree Subject and Relationship to the Labour Market

By the time that students come to 'choose' a course of study they have been subjected to a lengthy process of educational differentiation as a result of the interaction between important social characteristics such as gender, class, ethnicity and educational qualifications of considerable diversity. The choice of a higher education course is in itself the outcome of a process that can be termed 'pre-labour market segmentation'. As the labour market for graduates is segmented both horizontally and vertically (between job sectors that are more or less closed to only graduates with particular qualifications), the task of matching student backgrounds, aspirations and skills with particular labour markets lies at the heart of the role of degree courses in the labour market.

Entry to degree subjects is determined by prior qualifications. As a result of these 'tickets to entry' graduates are able to follow a subject/course of their 'choice'. However, it is well known that most females do not follow the science/maths/engineering route to higher education, preferring to follow the arts route. This has implications for their labour market relationship and the type of employment area they will enter. Also, women who do follow the non-traditional route/subjects will find themselves in a more favourable labour market situation not only than their traditional female counterparts, but also than those male graduates who follow arts-based subjects. This is because certain types of degree subjects are more in demand by employers than others. The HELM data show that those women who follow non-traditional subjects have a better labour market relationship than male graduates from the more arts-based subjects. However, these women do not have the same relationship to the labour market as their male counterparts who have followed the same subjects.

Subject Areas

Throughout this chapter only those courses that are common to both the 1982 and 1985 surveys have been examined (and only polytechnic and college courses have been used for cross cohort analysis because university graduates were included only in 1985). The outcome is that 17 courses were selected which were then categorized into different subject/course types in accordance with the Graduate Model (see Brennan and McGeevor, 1988). The 17 courses can be distributed between the three categories described below.

The first of these is the 'discipline based', which contains courses with little explicitly vocational content. They have a diffuse relationship to the labour market. The graduates from this category possess general skills and knowledge of value to employment, but not to any specific occupational role. These subjects have no special standing either in relation to training or in the regulation of entry to particular occupations. The degrees may have value across large parts of the labour market, the potential choices for their graduates are wide.

The second category is called 'thematic/vocational'. These are subjects which are vocational, but not in a highly specific way. Their relationship to the labour market is less diffuse than the discipline category. They have most of the features of the discipline-based courses, but in addition to general skills and knowledge the graduates also possess 'special' skills and knowledge applicable to 'being employed'. There is an element of occupational training in this type of degree in that graduates acquire some work-related skills that they may be able to use in a job, but like those graduates in the discipline-based category the process of job training begins with graduation.

In the third category, 'vocational/professional', subjects lead directly into a specific employment field. Graduates here have a close tie to a particular kind of employment. Possession of this kind of degree implies at least partial training for a job and a qualification that will have some regulatory relevance in determining entry. Degrees of this type will normally carry with them some form of professional recognition of completed or partially completed training. The choice of career occurs before entry to higher education, not after. Following graduation there are likely to be clearly defined steps towards acquiring full professional status and a job.

The seventeen courses can be roughly categorized as follows:

Discipline Based

- Biology
- Fine Art
- Humanities
- Modern Languages
- Combined Science

Thematic

- Graphic Design
- Social Science
- Textile and Fashion
- Business Studies
- 3D Design
- Communication Studies
- Economics

Vocational

- Accountancy
- Law
- Estate Management
- Electrical Engineering
- Computing

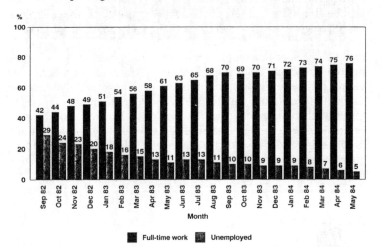

Figure 5.1a: Speed of entry into the labour market wave two, 1982 panel

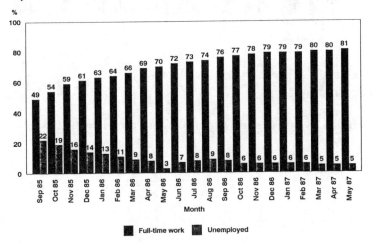

Figure 5.1b: Speed of entry into the labour market wave one, 1985 panel

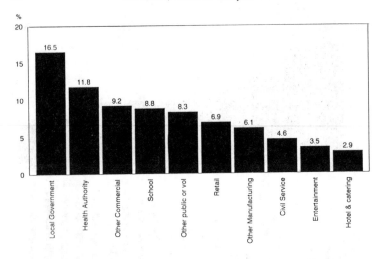

Figure 5.2a: Type of employing organisation wave two, 1982 panel – women

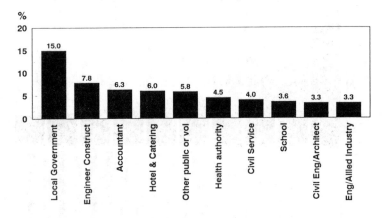

Figure 5.2b: Type of employing organisation wave two, 1982 panel – men

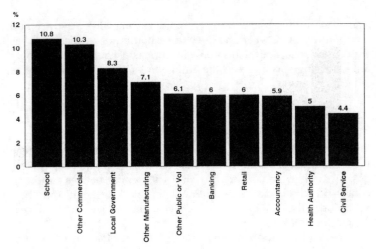

Figure 5.2c: Type of employing organisation wave one, 1985 panel – women

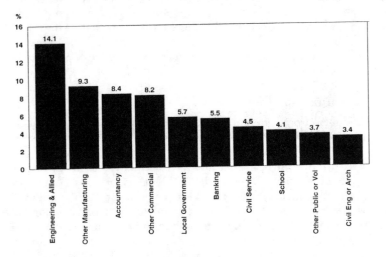

Figure 5.2d: Type of employing organisation wave one, 1985 panel – men

The location of subjects in the typology is somewhat arbitrary, and the boundaries between the categories should not be considered as rigid. They reflect differences only in emphasis. The categories imply an increasing specificity in the employment outcomes of a degree subject.

Speed of Entry into the Labour Market

Overall, the 1985 graduate cohort display quicker entry into the labour market, with the 1982 cohort having higher levels of unemployment. This could simply reflect differences between the two cohorts in labour market conditions. As stated earlier, it could be a reflection of the way 1982 was a 'bad' year and 1985 was a 'good' year for graduate employment.

Figure 5.1. shows that, three months after graduation, 42 per cent of the 1982 panel and 49 per cent of the 1985 panel were employed. However, the difference between the two panels increases six months after graduation, with 49 per cent of the 1982 panel and 60 per cent of the 1985 panel in employment. Then, the gap between the two cohorts narrows so that nearly two years after graduation the difference is only four per cent. The following analysis will attempt to explain the initial difference in the speed of entry into a paid job.

Type of Employment

Graduates from different cohorts enter different types of employment, reflecting the differing labour market conditions.

The data in Figure 5.2. have been presented so that the 'top ten' types of employing organisations have been arranged in descending order of popularity. Thus, for the 1982 female graduates the number one employing organisation is 'local government' (16.5%) followed by 'health authority' (11.8%). Both are public sector organisations, as are the top five employing organisations for men in the 1982 cohort except for 'other commercial' in third position (9.2%). This predominance of women graduates employed in the public sector and people-centred occupations is also reflected in the 1985 cohort. Here 'school' is the number one employing organisation (10.8 per cent), 'other commercial' second (10.3 per cent) and 'local government' third (8.3 per cent). The additions to the 1985 cohort are 'banking' and 'accountancy', replacing 'hotel and catering' and 'entertainment'.

For the male graduates of both the cohorts, the types of employing organisation differ from those of their female counterparts. The majority of the occupations are 'commercial', with the exception of

Table 5.3: Employment status two years after graduation by course and gender: wave two, 1982 panel

DEGREE SUBJECT	PAID JOB		FT STUDY		UNEMPLOYED		NOT AVAILABLE		OTHER	
	M	F	M	F	M	F	M	F	M	F
Biology	77.8	78.9	17.5	12.1	3.2	3.0	0.0	3.0	1.6	3.0
Fine Art	53.3	75.0	0.0	0.0	40.0	12.5	0.0	4.2	6.7	12.5
Humanities	65.2	75.5	4.7	7.0	23.3	12.3	2.3	1.0	4.7	4.2
Modern Languages	75.0	89.6	8.3	4.2	8.3	4.2	0.0	0.0	8.3	11.1
Science	74.2	66.7	19.0	13.9	5.2	11.1	0.0	5.6	1.7	25.0
Economics	90.0	62.5	5.0	0.0	5.0	25.0	0.0	12.5	0.0	24.4
Social Science	75.0	58.5	8.3	2.4	11.1	24.4	2.0	9.8	2.8	6.7
Graphics	89.6	83.4	0.0	3.3	6.9	6.7	0.0	6.7	3.4	2.8
Textiles	100.0	88.8	0.0	5.6	0.0	2.8	0.0	0.0	0.0	0.0
Business	95.5	88.0	0.0	4.0	0.0	0.0	0.0	4.0	4.5	15.4
3D Design	81.8	76.9	9.1	7.7	0.0	15.4	4.5	0.0	4.5	3.6
Communications	90.4	92.9	3.8	0.0	7.7	3.6	0.0	0.0	0.0	0.0
Accountancy	73.3	85.7	0.0	14.3	19.2	0.0	0.0	0.0	4.5	0.0
Law	78.6	93.3	7.1	0.0	0.0	0.0	14.3	6.7	0.0	0.0
Estate Management	92.3	100.0	0.0	0.0	0.0	0.0	0.0	0.0	7.7	0.0
Electrical Eng	93.1	100.0	6.9	0.0	0.0	0.0	0.0	0.0	0.0	0.0
Computing	100.0	100.0	0.0	0.0	0.0	0.0	0.0	0.0	0.0	0.0

'school' at number eight for both the 1985 (4.1%) and the 1982 (3.6 per cent) cohorts. The change for men is that the 1982 cohort has more in public sector organisations than the 1985 cohort, where more 'commercial' organisations are evident. This again reflects the different labour market situations of the two cohorts. One explanation for the prevalence of men in the public sector for the 1982 cohort is that when the labour market is unsteady, men will displace women from their jobs in so far as no appropriate jobs for men are available.

Size of Employing Organisation

The size of employing organisations follows a similar pattern for both the 1982 and 1985 cohorts. Also, there appears to be little difference when we compare male and female graduates within the same year (see Figure 5.3).

The most interesting development is that women electrical engineers from 1982 are all in organisations that employ between 50 and 199 people, whereas in the case of comparable graduates in the 1985 cohort, there are far more women in organisations employing over 500 people than for any other category. This suggests that more women in the 1985 cohort have been recruited by the larger firms. This is also a reflection of the differing labour market conditions between the two cohorts. In 1982 graduates experienced difficulty in gaining employment all round, and the women electrical engineers could only gain employment in the smaller companies, whereas more of their male counterparts for the same year were employed in organisations employing over 500 people than in any other category. This may be linked to the recruitment practices of companies. It should also be noted that the number of women graduates in engineering in the 1982 cohort was very small.

Do men tend to be in larger employing organisations in the case of all vocational subjects? If we look at computing and compare men and women within the same year (1982), we see that men predominate in companies of over 500 while women have a far higher tendency to be in companies with less than 20 employees (no males are represented in this latter category). To some extent, this can be explained by the large numbers of male graduates in the public sector organisations which are large organisations, or by the way large employers are regarded as providing better career prospects for graduates and so the most sought after jobs. A similar trend appears for the 1985 cohort in that more men than women are employed in the companies with over 500 employees. However, in this year fewer women than in the 1982 cohort are in organisations of less than 20.

Table 5.4: Employment status two years after graduation by course and gender: wave one, 1985 panel

DEGREE SUBJECT	PAID JOB		FT STUDY		UNEMPLOYED		NOT AVAILABLE		OTHER	
	M	F	M	F	M	F	M	F	M	F
Biology	76.2	75.3	19.0	21.3	4.8	2.2	1.2	1.1	6.4	0.0
Fine Art	61.8	59.6	11.8	14.9	17.6	21.4	2.9	2.1	5.9	2.1
Humanities	65.9	76.7	12.2	4.7	17.0	6.9	13.3	11.6	0.0	0.0
Modern Languages	87.0	89.4	7.4	7.6	5.6	3.0	0.0	0.0	0.0	0.0
Science	84.3	87.2	9.8	6.4	2.0	4.2	2.0	0.0	2.0	2.1
Economics	87.1	85.2	6.5	3.7	6.5	7.5	0.0	3.7	0.0	0.0
Social Science	71.4	85.2	10.2	8.2	16.2	3.3	0.0	3.3	2.0	0.0
Graphics	87.0	90.0	0.0	4.0	10.8	2.0	2.2	2.0	0.0	2.0
Textiles	66.7	80.2	9.5	5.8	23.8	9.3	0.0	3.5	0.0	1.2
Business	91.7	94.2	6.7	0.0	1.7	2.8	0.0	2.8	0.0	0.0
3D Design	88.5	65.1	3.8	11.6	7.7	13.9	0.0	7.0	0.0	2.3
Communications	81.8	85.7	4.5	5.4	13.6	5.4	0.0	1.8	0.0	1.8
Accountancy	96.4	96.0	0.0	4.0	3.3	0.0	0.0	0.0	0.0	0.0
Law	74.5	71.4	14.9	8.9	2.1	16.1	2.1	1.8	6.4	1.8
Estate Management	98.9	95.8	1.1	0.0	0.0	4.2	0.0	0.0	0.0	0.0
Electrical Eng	86.7	94.4	8.3	0.0	4.1	5.6	0.0	0.0	0.8	0.0
Computing	95.3	93.4	2.4	0.0	1.2	4.9	1.2	0.0	0.0	1.6

The general point here is that good labour market conditions seem to relate to the high percentage of graduates recruited into larger firms. It seems that the more favoured graduates (white/male/1985) are in the larger firms.

Employment Status and Type of Degree

Employment status is an important indicator of labour market success. If we compare employment status and degree subject, we can see that degree subject, irrespective of year of graduation, has the same relative labour market position. This section will show that labour market success is dependent upon the degree subject undertaken and graduate characteristics regardless of labour market conditions. There is a difference in labour market participation associated with the degree studied and the year of graduation (see Table 5.4.).

The vocationally specific subject category had the highest number of graduates in paid jobs for both cohorts in all waves. Interestingly, the graduates from this subject category that had the highest overall employment rate are women in 1982, with 100 per cent employment rate for estate management, electrical engineering and computing graduates. Male computing graduates in 1982 also had 100 per cent employment rate. However, in 1985 male and female graduates in this subject had equal employment rates, with both decreasing slightly from the high rates enjoyed by the 1982 graduates. This decrease in the numbers in employment is partly because there was an increase of graduates entering full-time study in 1985 from this subject category. In 1982 few of the graduates were in full-time study. Of those that were in full-time study, the numbers were equal for men and women. The graduates undertaking full-time study were mainly law and accountancy graduates, who need to study for professional qualifications. In 1985 more graduates from this subject category compared with the 1982 cohort went on to full-time study. The number of women in full-time study decreased in comparison with their 1982 counterparts, while the number of men in full-time study increased across all the subjects in the category.

Vocationally specific graduates have low rates of unemployment. Indeed, in 1982 no women graduates were unemployed from this category. The unemployed were male accountants, but in small measure in comparison with graduates from the other categories. In 1984 there are slight increases in employment for both men and women graduates.

Discipline-based graduates are at a disadvantage compared with their counterparts from the other subject categories. Their degrees have a much less explicit vocational content. As a result, these graduates do not enter a narrow range of specialist jobs, although there may be many areas of employment potentially open to them. It is not surprising to discover that this category has the highest levels of unemployment. There is a possibility that these graduates are deciding what they want to do, whereas with the other categories the decision has already been made by the choice of degree subject. The discipline-based graduates are likely to apply for jobs that do not require any specific degree, and the competition for such posts is likely to be very fierce. They may go on to further study to gain the qualifications needed for a specific employment area or to defer the decision about careers or just to enjoy the discipline and to continue studying.

In 1982 more men than women from this category were in full-time study, with science graduates having the highest numbers. For the 1985 graduates, the number of women in full-time study greatly increased, although there were still more men than women in full-time study. For both men and women, biology graduates were the highest number in full-time study in 1985.

It is important to note that male graduates from this category had the highest overall unemployment across all subject categories and cohorts. Fine art is the degree subject that has the highest unemployment rate overall in 1985 and for men in 1982. Unemployment overall for graduates from the discipline-based category fell slightly in 1985, with more men being unemployed than women.

More discipline based graduates were in paid jobs in 1985, reflecting more favourable labour market conditions. Female modern language graduates had the highest employment rates across both cohorts. For male graduates the highest employment rates were for biology in 1982 and economics in 1985.

Vocationally diffuse degrees contain most of the features of the discipline-based subjects, but as well as possessing general skills and knowledge, they provide specialist skills and knowledge applicable to certain areas of employment. In a sense, this category falls in the middle of the other two categories. This is reflected in the results gained.

In 1982, men from this category had the highest overall employment rate next to women graduates from the vocationally specific category. However, the degree subject that fares especially well is business studies. In 1982, male business studies graduates were second in their rate of employment to male textile graduates (the number of which is extremely small in our sample). An explanation is that business studies, while having a high vocational content, offers graduates the opportunity to apply their skills to a wide range of jobs. Also, commercial skills are required by a large number of graduate employers.

As for unemployment for this category of course, in 1982 there were more women unemployed than men. Male graduates from communications studies and women 3D Design graduates had the highest overall unemployment rates. By 1985, the pattern is reversed, with more vocationally diffuse men being unemployed, and with male textile graduates and women with degrees in 3D Design having the highest unemployment rates.

In 1982 there were more women than men in full-time study which helps explain why more men than women were in a paid job. By 1985 men had closed the gap for full-time study – but there were still more women in full-time study, and again they were the 3D design graduates.

An analysis across the subject categories highlights differences not only between the subject categories but also between cohorts. The highest proportion of graduates in paid jobs are, not surprisingly, from the vocationally specific category – and women have the highest employment rates. The lowest numbers of graduates in paid jobs are from the discipline-based subject category, although there was a slight increase in those gaining jobs within these degree subjects by 1985.

Overall, the discipline-based group has the highest numbers of graduates unemployed for all subjects in the category in 1982. But in 1985 male graduates in the vocationally diffuse group had the highest rate of unemployment. For women, the highest rate of unemployment is again for those graduates with discipline-based subjects.

Overall, the graduates with discipline-based degrees have the highest numbers in full-time study – for both cohorts. In 1982, more men than women were in full-time study; but in 1985 more women were in full-time study. The discipline-based category always has more men than women in full-time study; the vocationally diffuse category always has more women in full-time study; and the vocationally specific category has equal numbers of men and women in full-time study in 1982, but more men in full-time study in 1985.

We can conclude that year of graduation does affect the relationship of degree subject to the labour market. However, it appears that for most degree subjects, the difference between men and women remains constant regardless of the year of graduation. Labour market position is dependent upon the degree subject taken to a certain extent, but the characteristics of the graduates themselves play an important role in their relationship to the labour market. Women who have 'chosen' to study vocationally specific degree subjects are likely, in comparison with male graduates, to enjoy a prosperous relationship to the labour market. However, within subject groupings there are differences between men and women in their relationships to the labour market.

Along with the improvement in the overall labour market conditions and employment prospects for graduates, there appear to have been variations in fortunes between occupational areas and consequently between subject areas and courses. Some subjects/courses have been the target of greater employer demand leading to improved market conditions, options and opportunities, whereas other subjects/courses have not or, if anything, have been on the receiving end of diminished demand.

Chapter Six

Patterns of Graduate Destinations

Introduction and Summary

This chapter pursues further the theme of the previous two chapters by looking more closely at the patterns of graduate destinations. It explores in detail graduate labour market careers as the outcomes of a complex interaction between student choice of course, student social profiles, and labour market changes. It examines the possibility that some student characteristics are more conducive than others to success in the labour market, employment and career.

On the basis of the results of the survey of the 1985 panel of graduates carried out two years after graduation, the chapter explores in detail the links between (a) graduate destinations in terms of 'job type' and (b) graduate characteristics or 'graduate type'. Job types are distinguished with reference to information given by the 1985 panel about such matters as occupational rewards and work satisfaction; and graduate types are distinguished with reference to such matters as educational experience; social class identity; family background; and gender.

Consistent with what has been presented in previous chapters, it emerges that there are sizeable and significant variations in employment destinations according to, for instance, higher education subject/course and institution types. Thus, there is a strong tendency for each job type to draw its recruits from a relatively narrow range of subjects/courses, as well as a similar tendency for each to recruit from either universities or polytechnics and colleges. The issue of institutional differences will be returned to in Chapter Seven.

In that this applies to job types in general, then – given the evidence and analysis presented in previous chapters – we might expect the more rewarding and satisfying jobs to be occupied in something of a gender-biased manner. That is, higher education subjects/courses tend to display varying degrees of gender imbalances which are likely to carry over into job recruitment. As the following analysis shows, jobs vary considerably in terms of the proportion of incumbents who are women; and connectedly, there is a tendency for women to gravitate towards certain jobs rather than others.

Moreover, this picture is repeated when we look at other graduate social characteristics, such as educational experience prior to higher education; parental social class; and parental educational background.

It is clear from the evidence presented in this chapter, that graduates' characteristics established prior to – and so independently of – their higher educational experience play a crucial part in employment recruitment. The extent to which the gender factor continues to affect the career progression of women is illustrated by a series of comparisons between male and female graduates on the impact of family formation on income, employment status and geographical mobility.

Graduates find employment in a wide variety of occupations and, as we have seen, expect and hope for different things in their search for satisfying employment. Our first survey of 1985 graduates and diplomates used a multiple choice question to identify 57 types of 'job'. Thirty four of these employed more than 30 graduates and diplomates, and it is on these major job types that the following analysis concentrates.

For each type of job we look at who employers recruit, how they recruit, how much they reward and how satisfying the jobs are to the graduate recruits.

Job Recruitment Profile

The recruitment profile has several dimensions. First, there is the academic background of the recruits, both in terms of their subjects of study in higher education and their educational success at A-level and degree level. Second, there is gender and social background.

Recruitment to the major types of job by course is shown in Table 6.1. The courses that prepare graduates for each type of job are listed if they provide at least five per cent of the recruitment to that job area. (Where there has been a tie for fifth place those equal fifth have been listed.) The first percentage figure shows what proportion of the type of job was recruited from each type of course; the second percentage figure shows what proportion of the output of the subject area was working in this type of job. Thus, 13.9 per cent of general administrators had taken English or history at university, and 14.1 per cent of the output from such university courses were general administrators.

**Table 6.1: Recruitment from courses by major types of job
(wave one, 1985)**

		% Job Type	% Courses	No. of Cases
General Admin	Uni. Hist. Eng.	13.9	14.1	187
	BTEC Bus. Studies	8.0	16.5	(6.4%)
	Business Studies	8.0	14.3	
	Modern Langs	7.5	14.9	
	Combined Studies	5.3	17.2	
	Communication Studies	5.3	17.2	
	Economics	5.3	11.6	
Production	Mech. Engineering	17.9	6.1	30
Management	BTEC Bus. Studies	12.8	5.5	(1.3%)
	Uni. Mechanical Eng.	10.3	4.1	
	Textile Design	7.7	4.0	
	BTEC Computing	7.7	2.7	
Estate	Estate Management	86.7	83.5	128
Management				(4.4%)
Amenity	Sport	51.3	19.8	39
Management	Combined Studies	10.3	4.5	(1.3%)
	Biology Univ.	5.1	3.2	
	Hist. English Univ.	5.1	1.1	
Personnel	Business Studies	20.0	7.6	40
	Hist. English Univ.	12.5	2.7	(1.4%)
	Combined Studies	7.5	3.4	
	Communication Studies	7.5	5.2	
	Economics	7.5	3.5	
Retail	Hist. English Univ.	11.7	3.8	60
Management	Business	10.0	5.7	(2.0%)
	Economics	6.7	4.7	
	Textile Design	6.7	4.6	
	Economics Univ.	6.7	4.3	
	BTEC Mechanical Eng.	6.7	8.3	
Advertising	Graphic Design	20.9	11.3	43
	Hist. English Univ	14.0	3.3	(1.5%)
	Communication Studies	11.6	8.6	
	BTEC Business Studies	9.3	4.4	
	Economics Univ.	7.0	3.3	

**Table 6.1: Recruitment from courses by major types of job
(wave one, 1985) (continued)**

		% Job Type	% Courses	No. of Cases
Public Relations	Performing Arts	20.0	10.3	35
	Combined Studies	14.3	5.6	(1.2%)
	Sport	11.4	4.0	
	Social Science	8.6	4.2	
	Business Studies	5.7	1.9	
	BTEC Business Studies	5.7	3.4	
	Communication Studies	5.7	3.4	
System Analysis	Computing	28.7	24.7	115
	BTEC Computing	14.8	15.8	(3.9%)
	Computing Univ.	13.0	18.1	
	Electronic Engineering	6.1	5.9	
	Biology Univ.	5.2	12.5	
	BTEC Mechanical Eng.	5.2	12.5	
Programming	Computing	32.2	53.7	227
	BTEC Business	23.8	48.2	(7.7%)
	Computing Univ.	18.1	49.4	
Accounts	Accountancy	31.1	82.6	322
	Accountancy Univ.	23.3	87.2	(11.0%)
	Economics Univ.	10.2	35.9	
	Economics	7.1	26.7	
	Business	6.8	21.0	
Banking	Economics Univ.	20.6	7.6	34
	Hist. English Univ.	11.6	2.2	(1.2%)
	BTEC Business Studies	8.8	3.3	
	Accountancy Univ.	8.8	3.5	
	Modern Languages	8.8	3.2	
	Business Studies	8.8	2.9	
	Economics	8.8	3.5	
Other Finance	Economics Univ.	17.6	17.6	91
	Economics	13.2	14.0	(3.1%)
	Hist. English Univ.	8.8	4.3	
	BTEC Business Studies	8.8	8.8	
	Modern Languages	8.8	3.2	
Legal Services	Law	80.3	71.1	61
	Hist. English Univ.	4.9	1.6	(2.1%)
	Combined Studies	4.9	3.4	

Table 6.1: Recruitment from courses by major types of job
(wave one, 1985) (continued)

		% Job Type	% Courses	No. of Cases	
Other	Business Studies	19.4	26.7	144	
Management	BTEC Business Studies	9.0	14.3		(4.9%)
	Modern Languages	6.9	10.6		
	Combined Studies	5.6	10.6		
	Computing	5.6	5.6		
	Sport	5.6	7.9		
	Economics Univ.	5.6	8.7		
Science	Biology	47.4	32.5	78	
Research	Biology Univ.	20.5	25.4		(2.7%)
	Sciences	12.8	14.1		
Engineering	Electrical Engineering	31.8	17.6	66	
R&D	Communication Studies	30.3	17.5		(2.2%)
	Mechanical Eng. Univ.	16.7	17.5		
	BTEC Computing	6.1	3.6		
Engineering	Electrical Engineering	37.2	35.3	113	
Design	Mechanical Engineering	29.2	28.9		(3.9%)
	Mechanical Engineering	10.6	12.2		
	BTEC Mechanical Eng.	7.1	16.7		
Production	Mechanical Engineering	37.7	17.5	53	
Engineering	Mechanical Eng. Univ.	28.3	15.3		(1.8%)
	BTEC Computing	11.3	5.4		
	BTEC Mechanical Eng.	7.5	8.3		
Architecture	Architecture	61.9	76.5	21	
	Quality Surv.	19.0	4.3		(0.7%)
	3D Design	19.0	6.2		
Surveying	Quantity Surveying	75.0	65.2	80	
	Estate Management	18.8	11.3		(2.7%)
Laboratory	Technicians Biology	57.1	24.6	49	
Technicians	Sciences	16.3	11.3		(11.7%)
	Biology Univ.	14.3	11.1		
Other	Electrical Engineering	22.0	22.7	123	
Engineering	Mechanical Eng. Univ.	17.9	22.4		(4.2%)
	Mechanical Engineering	12.2	13.2		
	Quantity Surveying	10.6	14.1		
	Computing Engineering	8.1	12.0		

Table 6.1: Recruitment from courses by major types of job
(wave one, 1985) (continued)

		% Job Type	% Courses	No. of Cases
Teaching	Education	36.2	90.2	301
	Hist. English Univ.	13.0	21.2	(10.3%)
	Modern Languages	7.6	24.5	
	Sport	6.0	17.8	
Social/Welfare	Social Science	41.1	33.8	58
	Communication	10.3	10.3	(2.0%)
	Hist. English Univ.	10.3	3.3	
	Humanities	6.9	9.1	
	Law	5.2	4.3	
	Sport	5.2	3.0	
Journalism	Hist. English Univ.	46.7	7.6	30
	Communication Studies	13.3	6.9	(1.0%)
	Performing Arts	6.7	2.9	
	Textile Design	6.7	2.7	
Acting/Music/ Sport	Performing Arts	60.6	29.4	33
	Sport	24.2	7.9	(1.1%)
Broadcasting	Communication	25.0	12.1	28
	Graphic Design	14.3	5.0	(1.0%)
	Hist. English Univ.	14.2	2.2	
	Fine Art	10.7	8.8	
	Performing Arts	10.7	4.4	
Art & Design	Graphic Design	34.4	58.8	129
	Textile Design	33.3	57.3	(4.4%)
	3D Design	19.4	38.5	
	Fine Art	8.5	32.4	
Other Creative	Performing Arts	18.4	10.3	38
	Graphic Design	13.2	6.3	(1.3%)
	Hist. English Univ.	13.2	2.7	
	Textile Design	10.5	5.3	
	3D Design	10.5	6.2	
	Modern Languages	10.5	4.3	
Clerical	Hist. English Univ.	9.4	2.7	53
	BTEC Business Studies	9.4	5.5	(1.8%)
	Humanities	9.4	11.4	
	Modern Languages	9.4	5.3	
	Sport	7.5	4.0	
	Accountancy	7.5	3.3	

Table 6.1: Recruitment from courses by major types of job
(wave one, 1985) (continued)

		% Job Type	% Courses	No. of Cases
Secretarial	Hist. English Univ.	29.6	4.3	27
	Modern Languages	25.9	7.4	(.9%)
	Communication	7.4	3.4	
	Humanities	7.4	4.5	
Retail Sales	Hist. English Univ.	13.0	3.3	46
	BTEC Business Studies	10.9	5.5	(1.6%)
	Economics	13.0	7.0	
	Social Science	6.5	4.2	
	Modern Languages	6.5	3.2	
	Communication	6.5	5.2	
Other Non-	Hist. English Univ.	9.3	2.2	43
Management	Performing Arts	9.3	5.9	(1.5%)
	Science	7.0	4.2	
	Modern Languages	7.0	3.2	
	Humanities	7.0	6.8	
	Economics	7.0	3.3	

An indication of the diversity of recruitment can be gained by looking at the number of recruits drawn from any five course types. Table 6.2. presents this information. Thus, architecture, art and design, legal services and surveying all recruit from a small number of course types. But clerical, retail management and general administration recruit from a wide number of course types. Accountancy is often given as an example of a type of job open to all graduates regardless of subject matter. However, in our sample 79 per cent of recruits were drawn from five subject areas – a more narrow catchment than systems analysis and computer programming.

Table 6.3. shows the percentage of employees in each type of job who had attended a university, polytechnic or college of higher education. University graduates made up 21 per cent of employees in these 34 areas, but 52 per cent of those employed as journalists, 47 per cent of those employed in banking and 45 per cent of accountants. Colleges of higher education contribute 13 per cent of the workforce but 41 per cent of those working in acting, music or sport, 40 per cent of those in artistic design and 29 per cent of teachers.

Table 6.2: Percentage of recruits to major types of job
recruited from five course types

	Proportion from Five Course Types (%)	Rank Order
General Administration	43	32
Production Management	56	27
Estate Management	94	6
Amenity Management	74	15
Personnel	55	28
Retail Management	42	33
Advertising	63	23
Public Relations	60	24
Systems Analysis	68	20
Programming	74	16
Accounts	79	12
Banking	59	25
Other Finance	57	26
Legal Services	95	3
Other Management	47	30
Science Research	87	11
Engineering R&D	89	8
Engineering Design	88	10
Production Engineering	89	9
Architecture	100	1
Surveying	95	4
Laboratory Technician	94	5
Other Engineering	71	18
Teaching	67	21
Social Welfare	74	18
Journalism	77	13
Acting/Music/Sport	94	6
Broadcasting	75	14
Art and Design	96	2
Other Creative	66	22
Clerical	45	31
Secretarial	74	17
Retail Sales	50	29
Other Non-Management	40	34

Table 6.3: Type of educational institution attended by type of job

Type of Job	Educational Institution			
	Poly. (%)	Univ. (%)	CHE (%)	All
General Administration	67	25	9	188
Production Management	65	18	18	40
Estate Management	92	2	6	133
Amenity Management	69	15	15	39
Personnel	76	17	7	42
Retail Management	61	25	15	61
Advertising	71	21	9	44
Public Relations	77	17	6	35
Systems Analysis	72	25	3	114
Programming	76	20	4	233
Accounts	48	45	7	328
Banking	47	47	6	34
Other Finance	62	30	8	93
Legal Services	88	8	4	74
Other Management	76	15	9	149
Science Research	71	23	7	93
Engineering R&D	67	20	13	69
Engineering Design	77	14	9	118
Production Engineering	65	28	7	57
Architecture	84		16	31
Surveying	77	2	21	82
Laboratory Technicians	69	14	16	49
Other Engineering	65	26	9	126
Teaching	54	17	29	327
Social/Welfare	66	15	19	62
Journalism	38	52	10	29
Acting/Music/Sport	56	3	41	39
Broadcasting	63	13	25	32
Art and Design	60	1	40	134
Other Creative	67	14	19	43
Clerical	67	16	16	55
Secretarial	64	29	7	28
Retail Sales	57	17	26	46
Other Non-Management	62	21	17	42
Thirty four types average	**66**	**21**	**13**	**3070**

Table 6.4: 1985 Graduates two years after graduation.
Type of job by A-level point score and percentage
of firsts or upper seconds

Type of Job	Mean A-level Score	Firsts or Upper Seconds %
General Administration	6.8	38
Production Management	9.1	47
Estate Management	6.7	19
Amenity Management	5.3	26
Personnel	7.2	45
Retail Management	6.5	30
Advertising	7.1	40
Public Relations	6.0	46
Systems Analysis	7.2	46
Programming	6.7	46
Accounts	8.9	40
Banking	8.2	45
Other Finance	7.0	43
Legal Services	7.0	32
Other Management	6.7	39
Science Research	6.2	60
Engineering R&D	8.1	42
Engineering Design	6.3	41
Production Engineering	8.6	41
Architecture	6.4	45
Surveying	6.4	20
Laboratory Technician	5.2	23
Other Engineering	6.7	38
Teaching	6.6	44
Social/Welfare	6.0	38
Journalism	10.1	72
Acting/Music/Sport	6.0	36
Broadcasting	4.9	19
Art and Design	5.6	54
Other Creative	6.5	40
Clerical	6.5	35
Secretarial	7.4	30
Retail Sales	6.1	16
Other Clerical	6.6	26
All	**6.9**	**41**

Table 6.4. shows the average A-level score for each type of job and the proportion with Firsts and Upper Seconds. There is a difference between the broadcasting and journalism branches of the media. While journalists in our sample had the highest A-level score (10.1%) and the highest proportion of 'good degrees' (72%), broadcasting had the lowest A-level score (4.9%) and the second lowest proportion of good degrees (19%).

Highest A-level scores are found in journalism, production management and accountancy, lower scores in broadcasting, laboratory technicians and amenity management. A high proportion of good degrees are found in journalism, science research and art and design. There are low proportions of good degrees in retail sales, broadcasting and estate management.

Job Recruitment and Social Background

Jobs vary in the proportion of women employed. In our sample women were only four per cent of production engineers but 96 per cent of secretaries. The first column of Table 6.5. shows the percentage of women in each job type. This same information is given in rank order in Table 6.6. Thus, Table 6.6. shows secretarial work as 1 per cent (having the highest proportion of women) and production engineering as 34 per cent (having the lowest).

Tables 6.5. and 6.6. also show different aspects of social background; the percentage who attended a fee paying school; the percentage whose fathers were senior professionals, managers or owners of large businesses; the percentage whose fathers were 'normal workers'; and the percentage whose fathers or mothers were graduates.

If the rankings for having a graduate mother and father are combined, then the types of jobs with the highest proportion of second generation graduates are acting, public relations, broadcasting, banking and journalism. The jobs with the lowest proportions from graduate backgrounds are personnel, laboratory technicians, engineering design and science research. As one might expect, there is an overlap between parental education and occupational status. If the rankings of fathers with senior professional or managerial occupations are combined with the rankings of fathers who are/were graduates then the types of job with the most socially elite backgrounds are journalism, banking, architecture, estate management and broadcasting. The least elite are science research, social welfare, teaching and programming.

Table 6.5: Type of job by social background 1985 cohort (percentages)

	Female (%)	Fee Paying School (%)	Father Profess (%)	Father Manual (%)	Father Graduate (%)	Mother Graduate (%)
General Administrat	58.6	17.6	36.9	16.0	23.5	14.4
Production Management	23.1	23.1	43.6	15.4	25.6	7.7
Estate Management	39.1	36.7	38.3	5.5	27.3	12.5
Amenity Management	56.4	20.5	43.6	20.5	30.8	12.8
Personnel	72.5	7.5	30.0	22.5	12.5	5.0
Retail Management	49.2	18.3	26.7	11.7	20.0	13.3
Advertising	55.8	27.9	34.9	7.0	18.6	9.3
Public Relations	74.3	28.6	37.1	11.4	31.4	17.1
Systems Analysis	26.1	12.2	29.6	13.9	20.9	13.0
Programming	27.8	9.3	25.6	20.7	18.1	9.7
Accounts	41.0	20.5	39.4	16.5	19.9	9.9
Banking	44.1	32.4	44.1	2.9	29.4	17.6
Other Finance	34.4	22.0	35.2	9.9	24.2	5.5
Legal Service	52.5	21.3	29.5	9.8	16.4	9.8
Other Management	47.9	18.1	35.4	6.3	24.3	11.8
Science Research	50.0	5.1	26.9	26.9	17.9	6.4
Engineering R&D	7.6	7.6	31.8	24.2	15.2	9.1
Engineering Design	7.1	6.2	31.0	20.4	13.3	8.8
Production Engineer	3.9	7.5	32.1	24.5	13.2	9.4
Architecture	33.3	23.8	42.9	4.8	19.0	4.8
Surveying	17.5	11.3	40.0	18.8	21.3	7.5
Lab. Technician	63.3	2.0	22.5	18.4	12.2	8.2
Other Engineer	14.6	15.4	29.3	18.7	16.3	9.8
Teaching	63.5	12.6	26.6	22.6	16.6	10.0
Social/Welfare	67.2	6.9	19.0	20.7	17.2	8.6
Journalism	55.2	33.3	50.0	0.0	33.3	13.3
Acting	51.5	24.2	42.4	15.2	30.3	21.2
Broadcasting	48.1	25.0	46.4	14.3	39.3	14.3
Art & Design	60.9	18.6	34.9	12.4	21.7	10.1
Other Creative	68.4	21.1	36.8	10.5	15.8	15.8
Clerical	57.7	9.4	32.1	17.0	22.6	7.5
Secretarial	96.3	14.8	29.6	11.1	29.6	14.8
Retail Sales	47.8	13.0	32.6	8.7	19.6	4.3
Other Non-Management	39.5	23.3	32.6	14.0	18.6	16.3

Table 6.6: Type of job by social background 1985 cohort
(rank order)

	Female (R)	Fee Paying School (R)	Father Profess (R)	Father Manual (R)	Father Graduate (R)	Mother Graduate (R)
General Administrat	9	19	12	15	12	7
Production Management	29	10	4	16	9	27
Estate Management	24	1	10	31	8	13
Amenity Management	11	15	5	8	4	12
Personnel	3	30	24	5	33	32
Retail Management	17	17	30	22	17	10
Advertising	12	5	16	29	22	22
Public Relations	2	4	11	23	3	3
Systems Analysis	28	24	26	20	16	11
Programming	27	27	32	6	23	20
Accounts	22	14	9	14	18	17
Banking	21	3	3	33	7	2
Other Finance	25	11	15	26	11	31
Legal Service	14	12	27	27	27	18
Other Management	19	18	14	30	10	14
Science Research	16	33	29	1	24	30
Engineering R&D	32	28	22	3	30	23
Engineering Design	33	32	23	9	31	24
Production Engineer	34	29	21	2	32	21
Architecture	26	8	6	32	20	33
Surveying	30	25	8	10	15	29
Lab. Technician	7	34	33	12	34	26
Other Engineer	31	20	28	11	28	19
Teaching	6	23	31	4	26	16
Social/Welfare	5	31	34	7	25	25
Journalism	13	2	1	34	2	9
Acting	15	7	7	17	5	1
Broadcasting	18	6	2	18	1	8
Art & Design	8	16	17	21	14	15
Other Creative	4	13	13	25	29	5
Clerical	10	25	20	13	13	28
Secretarial	1	21	25	24	6	6
Retail Sales	20	22	19	28	19	34
Other Non-Management	23	9	18	19	21	4

Table 6.7: Type of employer and salary

Employer	No.	Male Rank	Salary	No.	Female Rank	Salary
Civil Service	59	5	11,295	42	5	9,430
Local Government	72	3	10,776	74	2	10,177
University	19	15	10,806	15	13	8,668
Polytechnic	11	18	10,566	8	17	7,902
Technical College	9	19	10,991	11	15	8,985
School	52	6	10,564	115	1	10,353
Health Authority	15	16	8,524	39	7	8,394
Other Public	44	7	11,564	57	4	9,847
Civil Eng. Builder	22	13	13,910	6	19	13,000
Architect	67	4	13,085	25	8	11,128
Oil Mining	22	13	15,214	8	17	13,041
Chemical	28	9	13,104	14	14	10,578
Engineering	143	1	12,259	25	8	11,863
Engineering Consult.	17	16	13,661	3	*	*
Food, Drink, Tobacco	23	12	13,026	22	10	12,014
Gas, Elect., Water	13	17	11,659	6	19	10,603
Other Manufacturing	112	2	12,817	62	3	11,966
Accountant	27	10	11,993	4	*	*
Transport & Commis.	10	19	12,554	3	*	
Retail	6	22	15,401	16	12	11,555
Banks & Finance	26	11	14,665	20	11	12,445
Other Commercial	36	8	14,441	41	6	13,087

Gender, Family Formation and Career Progression

Women graduates, on average, earn less than men graduates. In our 1982 cohort it was £1,619 less: in our 1985 cohort the figure was £1,563. As we have seen, the most important influence on graduate earnings is course of study. However, in three quarters of our subject areas male graduates in full time employment earned more than female graduates.

Table 6.7. looks at male and female earnings in the 22 categories of employer that employed more than ten full-time graduates. The table shows the number of graduates, the rank order in terms of number (i.e., school is ranked as the first employer for women, accounting for 115 graduates, engineering is the first category for men, accounting for 143 graduates), and the average salary. For types of employer with less than five male or female graduates the average salary has been omitted. In all the categories where male and female income has been recorded, the male income is always the higher.

It is possible that the women working for the above listed employers were doing a different kind of job from the men. If we combine type of work and employer, 17 groupings with more than ten employees emerge. Because of the low number of female engineers and surveyors, and the low numbers of men working in the nursing/medical or social welfare area, there are only seven categories with more than five men and women. These are shown in Table 6.8.

Table 6.8: Earnings of male and female full-time employees by type of work and employer (1985 cohort three and a half years after graduation)

Type of Work	Employer	Income (£)	
		Male	Female
Teaching	School	10,563	10,435
Architecture	Architect	12,423	10,432
General Administration	Civil Service	11,060	8,270
Marketing Sales	Other Manufacturing	13,889	11,121
Systems Analysis	Other Manufacturing	14,504	12,983
General Administration	Local Government	10,979	9,233
Science Research	University	9,610	9,259

In each of these categories women still show lower earnings than men. A partial explanation for these differences might lie in the way finding a partner and starting a family affect the careers and the mobility of men and women differently. The evidence points to a situation where finding a partner appears to improve the career prospects of men, but reduce those of women graduates.

Six years after graduation 61 per cent of women and 53 per cent of men from the 1982 cohort described themselves as married or in a permanent relationship. Of the 1985 cohort, three years after graduation 48 per cent of the women and 39 per cent of the men were married or in a permanent relationship. What effect has this had on their careers? In the following brief analysis a division into three categories has been made between the graduates: those who are

Table 6.9: Employment status by stage of family
formation and gender

| | (1982 Cohort) | | | | | |
| | Single | | Partner/ No Children | | Children | |
	M	F	M	F	M	F
Full-time employee	82.0	83.8	87.5	81.4	80.4	42.0
Part-time employee	2.0	3.6	1.0	7.3	3.9	15.3
Self-employed	6.4	6.1	7.8	5.9	7.8	6.9
Full-time study	2.8	1.6	1.0	1.4	0.0	1.5
Unemployed	5.6	4.0	1.5	1.9	2.0	6.8
Family responsibility	0.0	0.0	0.5	0.9	5.9	26.7
Other	0.8	1.0	0.5	1.4	0.0	0.8

| | (1985 Cohort) | | | | | |
| | Single | | Partner/ No Children | | Children | |
	M	F	M	F	M	F
Full-time employee	81.9	76.4	87.8	80.1	77.6	40.0
Part-time employee	2.0	2.5	2.2	4.4	5.6	13.3
Self-employed	6.0	8.6	4.2	6.6	7.7	10.0
Full-time study	5.3	7.0	3.3	4.4	4.2	5.6
Unemployed	4.2	3.4	1.4	1.9	2.1	5.5
Family responsibility	0.2	0.6	0.0	0.0	2.8	23.3
Other	0.5	1.6	1.2	2.4	0.0	2.2

married with dependent children; those who are married or in a permanent relationship, but without dependent children; and the rest, referred to as 'single'.

Table 6.9. shows the employment status for men and women in each of these categories. The presence of dependent children increases the likelihood of men and women working part-time, or of not being in paid work. However, while for men 3.9 per cent (of the 1982 graduates) and 5.6 per cent (of the 1985 graduates) work part-time, the corresponding figures for women are 15.3 per cent and 13.3 per cent. Not being in paid work is the employment status of about a quarter of women with dependent children. For men with dependent children less than six per cent are not in employment. Unemployment appears to be most common amongst single men and amongst women with dependent children.

For those who remain in full-time employment, how does family formation affect earnings? Table 6.10. shows mean salaries for men and women in full-time employment according to their marital or family status. Men are here shown to have higher pay than women overall, but the difference is least amongst the 'single' and greatest for those with dependent children. For women, single women earn more than those with partners, who in turn earn more than those with dependent children. For men the opposite is true; single men earn less than those with partners or dependent children. A single woman earns on average 9 per cent *more* than one with dependent children. A single man earns 9 per cent *less* than one with dependent children.

Table 6.10: Mean salary of graduates in full-time employment by family formation

| | **(1982 Cohort)** | | |
	Single	Partner/ No children	Dependent children
Male	13,549	15,012	14,694
Female	12,422	11,960	11,385

| | **(1985 Cohort)** | | |
	Single	Partner/ No children	Dependent children
Male	12,708	13,201	13,473
Female	11,294	11,202	9,984

Why does marriage seem to help a man's career but hinder a woman's, even in the absence of dependent children? One partial explanation could be differing rates of geographical mobility. With many graduate jobs, career progression is dependent on the ability to move. Graduates were asked if they had moved county or city as a result of their work. The results show that while men have been slightly more mobile overall than the women, there are marked differences according to marital or family status. Thus single women are shown to be *more* mobile than single men. Acquiring a partner, however, which has only a slight effect on mobility of male graduates, has a marked effect on that of the women. Having dependent children reduces the mobility of both men and women; but again the effect on women is greater. This is illustrated in Table 6.11.

Table 6.11: Moving county or city as a result of work.
Male and female graduates by stage of
family formation (1982 and 1985 cohorts)

| | (1982 Cohort) | |
	Male	Female
Single	52.6	60.0
Partner/no children	51.6	42.9
Dependent children	29.7	18.0
All	48.0	43.2

| | (1985 Cohort) | |
	Male	Female
Single	46.9	49.1
Partner/no children	44.2	35.4
Dependent children	34.5	18.3
All	45.0	41.0

Graduates were also asked if they had moved county or city as a result of their partner's work. Here the results are even more striking. Table 6.12. shows that for the 1982 cohort in the six years since graduation, women with partners, but no dependent children, have been three times more likely than men to move area as a result of their partner's work.

Table 6.12: Moving county or city as a result of partner's work: male and female graduates by stage of family formation (1982 and 1985 cohorts)

	(1982 Cohort)	
	Male	Female
Single	0.0	0.0
Partner/no children	7.4	23.8
Dependent children	3.0	23.4
All	3.2	15.8

	(1985 Cohort)	
	Male	Female
Single	0.0	0.0
Partner/no children	11.2	23.5
Dependent children	2.9	25.0
All	4.3	12.9

The HELM data presented in this chapter point in the direction of a graduate labour market which is not merely horizontally segmented, but also vertically stratified. That is, the graduate labour market is characterised by an unequal spread of rewards and satisfactions associated with an unequal distribution of access and opportunities tied to graduates' subject choice, and through this to their background (pre-higher education) characteristics. To this must be added the effects of non-work features of graduates' lives – of which family commitments are generally most important. The point to emphaise is that all of these factors interact. The effect of any one factor taken in isolation is limited in comparison to the combination effect of all the factors which influence individual lives. This is as true of educational qualifications as it is of anything.

Chapter Seven examines the possibility that the stratified graduate labour market is also tied to a compounding stratified higher educational system.

The Stratified System of Higher Education

Introduction and Summary

The previous chapter pointed to the existence of a segmented graduate labour market and a stratified occupational system within which certain student characteristics and profiles are more conducive than others to a successful and satisfactory career. This chapter shifts the focus of attention by exploring the existence of a stratified system of higher education and the implications of such a system for the 'helm' relationship.

Within what was until very recently Britain's binary system of higher education, formal equivalence has been claimed between, on the one hand, the university sector and, on the other hand, the polytechnic and college sector. However, formal equality and 'quality control' do not necessarily guarantee comparability of student success in the labour market.

There is evidence of employers differentiating between institutions and institutional types – so that, for instance, university graduates are preferred relative to polytechnic graduates within the same subject area. Concomitantly, students/candidates discriminate between and within institutional types – enabling, for instance, universities to be more selective in their choice of course entrants. Given the association between (a) educational background and credentials prior to higher education course entry and (b) student/candidate social characteristics, it is not surprising to discover notable variations between and within institutional types with regard to student social profiles – distinguished in terms of, for instance, social class.

This chapter explores the presence of a system of informal stratification between and within institutional types – and in particular between the university and polytechnic sectors – which both feeds into and feeds off employer demand, graduate success and occupational stratification within the labour market. It is about the mutually supportive interplay between systems of stratification in both higher education and the labour market. Attention is paid to the implications for this interplay of the possibility that stratification specifically within the graduate labour market has in recent years become more marked. At the same time, the analysis acknowledges the pivotal importance of student orientations and social profiles within the 'helm' relationship, and so in influencing the future development of the interplay between higher educational stratification and labour market stratification.

The Context

Studies of employer attitudes show that a hierarchy exists in their preferences for graduates: a hierarchy partly determined by the esteem in which A-level grades are held as a 'screening' mechanism in recruitment. Non-university graduates are seen as less desirable recruits partly because their A-level profiles are lower than those of university students. The possession of a vocationally more relevant degree course is not necessarily seen to offset the absence of particular secondary school qualifications and having attended a non-university institution (Roizen and Jepson, 1985). On the assumption that employers look for two different kinds of skill in the recruitment of graduates – both technical specialist skills (of direct relevance to particular tasks) and more general social, personal and intellectual skills (of a transferable kind which are seen to make a graduate employee 'promotable' into varieties of management positions) – they are likely to look towards a more general profile of background qualifications and personal characteristics than that provided by the course and degree alone. The latter kind of skills will be sought especially in areas of employment where specialist vocational skills are not a requirement for the exercise of the job. For employers, a stratified education system can act as a 'screening device' to isolate candidates most likely to possess the desired characteristics. For many graduates, the recruitment policies of employees have the immediate effect of creating variations in the contact they are likely to have with employers whilst still in college. Early research has found a clear hierarchy in the percentages of graduates who found jobs with employers visiting institutions where employer preferences are reflected in the greater frequency with which they visit universities rather than polytechnics in search of employees (Boys and Kirkland, 1988). With the 'milk round' by employers to institutions being an important means of contact between final year students and employers, the process of finding a job begins in a manner loaded against polytechnic students (Boys *et al.* 1988).

Research points to a number of overall differences in the process of entry into the labour market between university graduates and polytechnic graduates. First Destination Statistics have consistently shown that among graduates from the same subject, university graduates are more likely than polytechnic graduates to be employed six months into employment (see Figure 7.1.a). They also show that differences between institution types in the rate of unemployment are more pronounced in the less 'vocational' subjects, which suggest that vocational elements of courses may provide some compensation

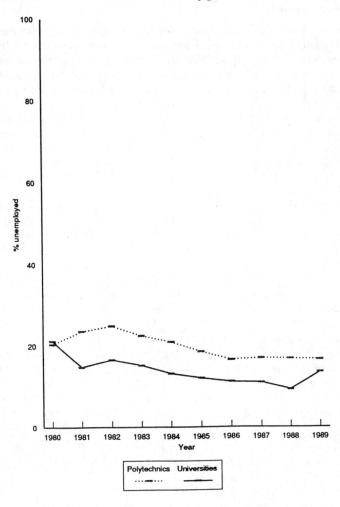

Figure 7.1a: Unemployed graduates: 6 months after graduation

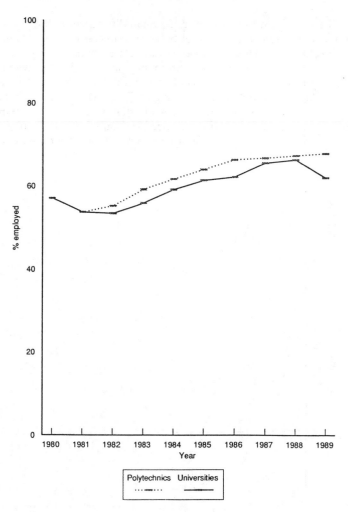

Figure 7.1b: Full-time employment: 6 months after graduation

for polytechnic graduates in areas where specific skills are required (Boys and Kirkland, 1988)(see Figure 7.1.b). University graduates are also more likely to go into further training or study than polytechnic graduates, which may further improve their more long-term career opportunities (see Figure 7.1.c). Boys and Kirkland's research also shows that Oxbridge graduates stand out in comparison to those from other universities, creating a more complex hierarchy of gradu-

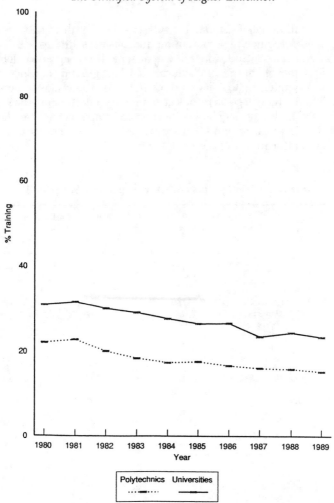

Figure 7.1c: Training and further education: 6 months after graduation

ate employability. This is reflected in the greater percentage of Oxbridge graduates that are employed by financial organisations in comparison with graduates both from other universities and from polytechnics.

The 1985 HELM graduate survey panel allows us to look in greater detail at institutional difference in both the social and educational characteristics and the labour market outcomes between graduates over a small range of comparable subject areas. For three subjects – mechanical engineering, computing and business studies – BTEC students are also included in the comparisons. This chapter will look first at some of the general educational background statistics of students by referring to A-level points and type of secondary schooling. The chapter will go on to look at employment destinations linked to institutional type, degree classification and student characteristics such as family background. Finally, we will look at graduates' perceptions of the quality of their employment.

Table 7.2: A-level points and O-level passes (1985 panel)

		9+ A-level (%)	6+ A-level (%)	Maths O pass (%)	English O pass (%)	(N)
Accountancy	CNAA	11	50	95	94	130
	University	88	95	100	99	95
Biology	CNAA	6	23	98	99	174
	University	73	92	99	99	89
Economics	CNAA	9	46	100	98	116
	University	79	95	98	96	128
Humanities	CNAA	7	34	57	94	87
History/English	University	82	87	94	99	286
Mechanical Eng.	CNAA	8	24	95	83	128
	University	63	74	95	97	116
	BTEC	*	*	93	89	90
Computing	CNAA	14	46	97	96	147
	University	47	71	98	96	94
	BTEC	*	*	90	87	134
Business Studies	CNAA	15	47	96	98	129
	BTEC	*	*	83	91	132

* BTEC diplomates were not asked their A-level point score.

Discussion

The clear and consistent pattern whereby polytechnic and college graduates take longer to get jobs than their university counterparts coupled with their higher rates of unemployment has to be accounted for. One obvious factor is educational success prior to higher education. Universities typically demand higher levels of performance in

GCE examinations. Table 7.2. presents the proportions of graduates and diplomates with nine or more A-level points; with six or more A-level points; and with O-level English language and mathematics. Ordinary level Mathematics and English are almost universal on all courses with the exception of Maths (for CNAA Humanities and, to a lesser extent, BTEC Business Studies) and English (for CNAA Mechanical Engineering).

The university courses have much higher proportions of their graduates with at least nine or at least six A-level points. There is, however, one interesting variation in course order. The CNAA computing graduates have a relatively high proportion with good A-level points – comparable with accountancy and business studies. The university computing graduates have a relatively low proportion – even less than mechanical engineering.

Table 7.3: Social background and secondary schooling (1985 panel)

		Grammar or Fee Paying School (%)	Fee Paying School (%)	Senior Prof. Father (%)	Manual Worker Father (%)	(N)
Accountancy	CNAA	37	15	42	20	130
	University	60	30	41	7	95
Biology	CNAA	29	5	27	25	174
	University	45	14	40	16	89
Humanities	CNAA	40	12	23	28	87
History/English	University	47	23	34	15	286
Mechanical Eng.	CNAA	25	5	27	19	128
	University	44	26	36	13	116
	BTEC	20	6	28	19	90
Computing	CNAA	39	6	32	15	147
	University	33	18	35	16	94
	BTEC	20	7	22	26	134
Economics	CNAA	28	13	27	22	116
	University	39	23	38	10	128
Business Studies	CNAA	51	21	36	12	129
	BTEC	37	22	30	13	132

* Weighted to reflect number of male and female graduates.

There are marked differences between institutions in terms of the social background of their students. The first column in Table 7.3. shows the proportions who attended a grammar, independent or fee paying school. Without exception, the BTEC diplomates have the lowest proportion with this background; and with only one exception, the university graduates have the highest proportion – the exception being computing.

The second column of Table 7.3. are subsets of the first column – the proportions who attended a fee paying school. Here a more consistent picture emerges. The university courses always have the

Table 7.4: Type of employment and category of employing organisation (1985 panel two years after graduation)

	Type of Employment (%)		Employer (%)	
Accountancy CNAA	Accountancy	81	Accountant	53
	Clerical	4	Banks & Finance	8
			Other Manuf.	6
Accountancy University	Accountancy	89	Accountant	72
	Banks	2	Banks & Finance	6
Biology CNAA	Science Research	29	Health Authority	22
	Lab. Technician	22	University	15
	General Admin.	7	Chemicals	9
Biology University	Science Research	23	Other Manuf.	16
	Accountancy	10	University	13
	Lab. Technician	10	Health	10
			Civil Service	10
			Other Commercial	10
Economics CNAA	Accountancy	28	Accountants	17
	General Admin.	11	Banks & Finance	14
	Other Finance	10	Local Government	12
Economics University	Accountancy	32	Accountants	28
	Other Finance	16	Banks & Finance	24
	General Admin.	9	Retail	5
Humanities CNAA	General Admin.	17	Other Public	18
	Teaching	13	Civil Service	16
	Clerical	11	Other Commercial	13
History/English University	Teaching	18	School	18
	General Admin.	13	Other Commercial	11
	Accountancy	10	Local Government	8
			Accountant	8
			Civil Service	8

Table 7.4: Type of employment and category of employing organisation (1985 panel two years after graduation) (continued)

	Type of Employment	(%)	Employer	(%)
Mechanical Engineering CNAA	Engineering Design	29	Engineering	54
	Engineering R&D	18	Other Manuf.	15
	Production Eng.	17	Engineering Cons.	8
Mechanical Engineering University	Other Engineering	21	Engineering	30
	Production Eng.	15	Other Manuf.	18
	Engineering Design	12	Accountant	8
Mechanical Engineering BTEC	Programming	18	Engineering	47
	Engineering Design	16	Other Commercial	9
	Production Eng.	10	Engineering Cons.	5
	Systems Analyst	10	Other Manuf.	5
Computing CNAA	Programmer	51	Other Commercial	27
	Systems Analyst	27	Other Manuf.	23
	Other Engineering	6	Other Engineering	16
Computing University	Programming	49	Other Manuf.	24
	Systems Analyst	18	Other Commercial	22
	Other Engineering	12	Engineering	11
Computing BTEC	Programming	50	Engineering	17
	Systems Analyst	16	Local Government	15
			Other Manuf.	13
Business Studies CNAA	Other Management	24	Other Manuf.	19
	Accountancy	21	Other Commercial	13
	General Admin.	14	Retail	10
Business Studies BTEC	General Admin.	15	Banks & Finance	14
	Other Management	13	Other Commercial	13
	Accountancy	10	Other Manuf.	12

* Weighted to reflect numbers of male and female graduates.

highest proportion, and the difference is significant in every case. The BTEC and CNAA comparisons are not significantly different.

The third column of Table 7.3. shows proportions whose fathers were either owners of large firms or businesses, senior professionals or senior managers. University graduates are more likely to have such a background, although the differences are only significant in the case of biology and humanities. The other significant difference is BTEC computing in that it has a lower proportion with this background than the equivalent CNAA or university courses.

The final column shows the proportions with fathers who are or (if retired were) manual workers. University graduates with such fathers display significantly lower proportions for accountancy, economics and history or English. BTEC computing is also significantly less than CNAA computing (but not university computing).

Is there any evidence that graduates from polytechnics and colleges have different labour market experiences compared with graduates from universities and BTEC diplomate holders?

The HELM data suggests that the subject of study has a greater influence than the type of institution, but that within each subject area (with the exception of computing) university graduates experience less unemployment and BTEC diplomates more unemployment than the CNAA graduates (see Figure 7.1.).

Table 7.4. lists the three most important types of employment and category of employer for each course. In terms of the broad categories used, courses on either side of the binary divide have similar destinations. However, there are differences at the margins. University accountancy graduates are more likely to be working as accountants *for* accountants. University biologists are less likely to be laboratory technicians and more likely to be recruited into accountancy or computing (about 12% become systems analysts or programmers compared to 3% of the CNAA biologists). They are also more likely to work in manufacturing than in the health service. University economics graduates are more likely to be accountants or in other financial employment and are less likely to be found in local government. A comparison of CNAA humanities graduates with university history and/or English graduates shows the university graduates to be more likely to go into teaching, accountancy and journalism. Seven per cent of history/English graduates became journalists; and 81 per cent of journalists had this academic background.

There are two distinct features of the destinations of mechanical engineering graduates and diplomates. First a significant proportion of university graduates (11%) work for accountants or banks and finance (none of the CNAA graduates have employers in these categories). Second, a large proportion of BTEC mechanical engineering diplomates work as programmers or systems analysts. CNAA and university computing graduates have a very similar job and employer profile, but the BTEC diplomates are unique in having local government as a major employer. BTEC business studies diplomates were more likely to be in routine clerical, secretarial or retail sales work than business studies graduates. These categories accounted for 12 per cent of the diplomates but less than two per cent of the graduates.

Table 7.5: Salary from principal occupation (1985 panel two years and three and a half years after graduation)

	1987	1988/89	Growth (%)	Proportion of CNAA 1987 (%)	Proportion of CNAA 1988/89 (%)
Accountancy CNAA	8,238	12,511	152		
Accountancy University	9,629	15,512	161	117	124
Biology CNAA	7,360	9,952	135		
Biology University	7,978	11,930	150	108	120
Economics CNAA	8,290	11,395	137		
Economics University	10,039	13,310	133	121	117
Humanities CNAA	7,681	10,324	134		
History/English University	7,985	10,745	135	104	104
Mechanical Engineering CNAA	9,955	12,574	126		
Mechanical Engineering University	10,148	13,441	132	102	107
Mechanical Engineering BTEC	9,627	12,090	126	97	96
Computing CNAA	10,487	15,199	145		
Computing University	11,006	14,638	133	105	96
Computing BTEC	8,981	12,625	141	86	83
Business Studies CNAA	9,523	13,477	142		
Business Studies BTEC	8,145	10,955	134	86	81

* To avoid distortions to the mean salary by very high or very low salaries outlying scores were recorded to the fifth and ninety-fifth percentile score. The 1987 figures have been weighted to reflect actual numbers of male and female graduates.

Two years after graduation, all university subject areas have higher average salaries than comparable CNAA courses. All BTEC subject areas have lower average salaries. Eighteen months later these differences have increased in all but two of the subject areas. For the rest, university graduates' earnings increase more quickly and BTEC diplomates' earnings increase more slowly than those of CNAA graduates (see Table 7.5.). The two exceptions are economics, where CNAA graduates narrow the gap slightly (although university graduates retain a 17% advantage), and computing, where CNAA graduates' earnings are greater than those of university graduates after three and a half years.

The status hierarchy among university graduates, CNAA graduates and BTEC diplomates appears to be pronounced and persistent. To what extent can this be explained by differences in degree classification and/or socio-economic background? Table 7.6. compares the medium salary of different subject areas two years after graduation. The panel has been sub-divided into those whose fathers are (or were) in high status employment (in senior professional or managerial employment or the owners of large firms or businesses) and those with a first or upper second degree or, in the case of BTEC diplomates, a distinction or merit. A high status background increases median salary by 28 per cent for humanities graduates; 14 per cent for BTEC business studies; and 11 per cent for CNAA business studies. However, in accountancy a high status background has the effect of *reducing* median salary – by 20 per cent for CNAA graduates and by seven per cent for university. Part of the explanation for this would

Table 7.6: Family background, degree classification*
and median salary after two years

	Prof./ Manag. (£'s)	Other Seg. (£'s)	Good Degree (£'s)	Other Degree (£'s)
CNAA Accountancy	6,528	8,163	8,882	7,207
University Accountancy	9,260	9,983	10,500	8,575
CNAA Biology	7,316	6,855	7,203	6,899
University Biology	7,750	7,900	8,717	7,324
CNAA Economics	8,000	8,310	8,055	8,213
University Economics	10,650	10,000	11,000	9,000
CNAA Humanities	9,100	7,135	8,414	7,294
University History/English	8,239	8,000	8,500	8,000
CNAA Mechanical Engineer	10,270	10,014	10,234	9,859
University Mechanical Engineer	10,700	10,500	10,923	10,000
BTEC Mechanical Engineer	8,500	9,634	9,100	9,252
CNAA Computing	10,740	11,250	11,894	10,700
University Computing	11,000	11,125	11,200	11,000
BTEC Computing	8,675	8,858	8,841	8,812
CNAA Business Studies	10,066	9,100	10,000	9,010
BTEC Business Studies	8,550	7,500	9,450	7,421

* Merit or distinction in the case of BTEC awards.

seem to be the factor of reduced pay during professional training. While 90 per cent of high status CNAA accountancy graduates are working as accountants, the figure for other social backgrounds is only 73 per cent. The figures for university accountancy graduates are 97 per cent and 84 per cent in the same direction.

When only those from high status backgrounds are considered, university graduates earn on average 13 per cent more than CNAA graduates, who in turn earn 17 per cent more than BTEC diplomates. The BTEC differential is fairly consistent, but there are major variations amongst university graduates. Thus, high status university accountancy and economics graduates earn, respectively, 42 per cent and 33 per cent more than high status CNAA graduates. The one exception is humanities graduates, where high status university graduates earn on average 9 per cent less. Among other status groups, university graduates have an overall 12 per cent advantage and BTEC diplomates a 15 per cent disadvantage.

A 'good' degree classification (or merit or distinction in the case of BTEC diplomates) increases the average earnings of most subject areas. The average improvement was 11 per cent. The benefit was most marked for BTEC business studies, university economics and accountancy and CNAA accountancy. The earnings effect of degree classification was negligible for university and BTEC computing, BTEC mechanical engineering and CNAA economics. The advantage of university graduates over CNAA graduates and their mutual advantage over BTEC diplomates persists regardless of degree classification. The most extreme variation is amongst economics Firsts and Upper Seconds. Here, the median salary for university graduates was 37 per cent higher than that for CNAA graduates.

Does a good classification with a CNAA degree earn more than a university degree that is not a First or Upper Second? This is the case in accountancy, humanities, mechanical engineering and computing (though in the latter case a good CNAA degree earns more than a good university degree). Only in business studies does a merit or distinction in a BTEC diploma earn more than a CNAA Lower Second or Third classification.

Two years after graduation, salary may be an important indicator of long-term employment success, but it is by no means the only one. Occupational status, intrinsic interest, skill level and the extent of training for future advancement mean future benefits as well as current satisfactions. Table 7.7. presents responses to a series of questions on these topics.

The first column shows the proportions who responded positively to the question 'Have you received any training that is directed towards future promotion and career development rather than to-

Table 7.7: Aspects of job quality and career development
(Those in paid employment from the 1985 panel)

	Career Dev. Tr'ng (%)	Trad. Grad. Job (%)	Deg. Ess'tl Entry (%)	Grad. Abil'y Req'd (%)	Long-Term Job (%)	Feel Over Qual'd (%)	(N)
Accountancy CNAA	68	47	39	52	62	23	125
Accountancy University	81	51	60	51	54	17	90
Biology CNAA	41	23	34	40	36	42	132
Biology University	42	32	39	36	24	42	74
Economics CNAA	44	25	31	40	50	42	101
Economics University	59	38	38	45	45	24	106
Humanities CNAA	37	20	18	28	29	56	61
History/English University	32	27	30	33	39	34	213
Mechanical Engineering CNAA	43	39	34	48	33	40	120
Mechanical Engineering University	61	35	48	51	44	34	105
Mechanical Engineering BTEC	42	**	**	**	47	29	66
Computing CNAA	32	38	34	55	38	20	138
Computing University	41	50	46	60	44	24	84
Computing BTEC	35	**	**	**	46	25	108
Business Studies CNAA	54	34	32	56	50	34	119
Business Studies BTEC	40	**	**	**	34	41	111
							1753

* Weighted to reflect numbers of male and female graduates.
** Question not included in BTEC survey

wards skills for your existing job?' This varies from 82 per cent for university accountancy to 32 per cent for university English or history and CNAA computing. The university graduates are substantially more likely to have received such training. Only in the case of biology and English/history/humanities is there less than a nine per cent gap between CNAA and university graduates. BTEC diplomates are (in the case of computing and mechanical engineering) as likely as CNAA graduates to receive such training, although an interpretation would be that training is to bring them up to graduate level. Fourteen per cent fewer BTEC diplomates than CNAA graduates in business studies had received such training.

Columns two, three and four of Table 7.7 show the responses to the question 'Would you describe your present job as 'graduate level employment' in the sense that (a) it has traditionally been regarded as such; (b) a degree is an essential requirement for entry into this area of employment; and (c) the inherent character of the work requires graduate level ability/training?' University graduates enjoy an advantage on each of these indicators. The only exceptions to this pattern are mechanical engineering, where three per cent more CNAA graduates thought they were in a 'traditional graduate job'; and accountancy and biology, where CNAA graduates are marginally more likely to consider that their work required graduate level abilities.

The final column in Table 7.7 gives a summary of the responses to the question 'Do you feel that you are over-qualified or under-qualified for the work that you do?'. University graduates in humanities and economics are considerably less likely to be in this position than CNAA graduates. In biology across the binary divide there is an equally high proportion of 42 per cent feeling overqualified. Only in computing are CNAA graduates less likely than university graduates to feel overqualified. The feeling of being overqualified for a job must rest in part on what graduates' qualifications are, so that the BTEC sample are not directly comparable. Nevertheless, 41 per cent of BTEC business studies diplomates felt overqualified.

The information presented in this chapter suggests that, with a few notable exceptions, subject area is far more important that level of qualification or the type of institution attended in determining which type of employment a graduate will end up in. However, the status hierarchy of qualifications found within education is reproduced in employment. Graduates from universities and polytechnics in any one subject are initially in similar types of employment, but university graduates have, on average, better jobs. Similarly, CNAA graduates have better jobs than BTEC diplomates. In two cases the hierarchy means that, in effect, they are not competing in the same labour market. These two cases are between (a) university and CNAA economics graduates and (b) business studies graduates and BTEC diplomates. In both cases the gap is considerable and suggests a segmented labour market and employment structure.

Polytechnics and colleges are recruiting more students with pre-entry characteristics that are not favoured in the labour market. Nevertheless, educational qualifications can compensate. A good class of degree in the right kind of subject will generally make a polytechnic graduate very employable, irrespective of background characteristics. Some polytechnic graduates do better in the labour market than university graduates. Some women graduates do better than men. Some working class graduates do better than middle or upper class graduates. It is the combination of factors which is most important.

Will university titles improve the employment prospects of graduates from the former polytechnics? Unless the changes of title lead to fundamental changes in the recruitment profiles and 'social catchments' of particular institutions, the evidence of this chapter suggests that improvements will be only minimal.

Chapter Eight

The Competent Graduate

Introduction and Summary

In the last few chapters, we have examined a process whereby students/graduates are channelled by virtue of their background, social characteristics and aspirations and by way of a 'stratified' higher educational system into a segmented labour market and associated 'stratified' occupational structure.

In this complex process of matching 'supply' with 'demand', the issue arises of how well this representation of the 'helm' relationship sits with the further possibility raised in the opening chapters of this book that higher educational institutions and courses are about – to some extent and perhaps increasingly by design – preparing students for prevailing employer demands for particular occupational skills and general graduate competences.

Questions arise concerning the possibility of identifying the characteristics and determinants of 'competency' and 'the competent graduate'; of unravelling the connection between graduate 'competences' and labour market segmentation and occupational stratification; of how far 'competences' are transferable between higher education and employment; how far 'competences' are transferable between types of employment; and the extent to which employment related 'competences' are dependent upon job experience and training. It is beyond the confines of this report to look at 'competency' from the point of view of employers. Instead, the graduates' own perceptions of the value of higher education in providing work-related skills will be examined. This chapter addresses issues raised by the responses of the graduates: issues which again bring to the fore some of the conflicts and contradictions which arise between the social and economic demands for higher education.

Changing expectations of higher education have raised a number of questions about the relevance to students and employers of curricula, course organisation and pedagogy as presently delivered. Traditional academic approaches of discipline specialisation that emphasise theoretical and conceptual learning rather than practical vocational application have come under criticism from a variety of sources as inadequate for the development of more general employment related skills. When, over the last decade, the concept of 'mismatch' between graduate supply and labour market demand has been invoked, it has been only to express concern over a shortage of graduates with particular types of degree qualifications. Employers have also detected a mismatch between the kinds of general and personal skills they are looking for in graduate recruits and the research and scholarship-orientated skills fostered by higher education. Employers treat the more general personal qualities of students as important, especially in the areas of communications, literacy and numeracy, but also as regards social and interactive skills (Pearson and Pike, 1989).

Since the publication by the National Advisory Body in 1986 of a document introducing the concept of 'transferable skills' into the debate on graduates and the labour market, growing attention has been given to this aspect of graduate 'employability' in the development work of various policy making organisations, exemplified by the Enterprise Initiative of the Training Agency and the Higher Education for Capability Project of the Royal Society of Arts. Most graduate occupations require broad work-related competences not confined to particular vocations or professions. In a continuously changing labour market, tightening the bond between higher education and employment has been seen to mean not only the provision of enough specialist vocational skills to fill labour market 'slots', but also the creation of a work force which is *generally* competent and flexible enough to be able to change and adapt to shifting labour market requirements. Since the first HELM report was published a great deal of debate has taken place on the role of competence training in higher education, and many course leaders have begun to look at ways in which general skills training can be more firmly emphasised and integrated into the curriculum (Lyon, 1988).

From the point of view of employers, transferable skills, being common to many jobs, could and should be taught outside particular jobs and professions. The mastery of 'general skills' is an expected outcome of higher education, whatever the degree specialism. One of the key roles of higher education in the preparation for employment is seen to lie in the creation of conditions for making graduates generally competent, through the fostering of skills that are 'transferable' between one job situation and another. Such skills are not vocational, but vocationally related, and most higher education courses claim to foster them, albeit in a vague and unspecified way. The possession of a degree creates expectations about a person's abilities, although employers and professional organisations may, and do, use evidence other than degree status to indicate graduate-type skills, such as number and type of secondary school qualifications, work experience, and extra curricular activities (Pearson, 1976; Bradshaw, 1985).

Not all graduates from non-vocational courses are truly 'generalists', and a humanities graduate with few numeracy skills may not be 'employable' in as many different situations as, for example, a business studies graduate with *both* literacy and numeracy skills. The absence of basic skills from secondary school easily gets carried through into higher education and work, unless a profession or vocation sets up an extra entry requirement. This recently happened in the teaching profession, where O-level Maths was demanded of entrants to teacher training. There is some evidence to indicate that graduate employers show some preference for candidates with O-level Maths (Morgan and Scott, 1987). As was shown in Chapter Three, the curricular coverage to which each student is exposed during his or her educational career up to and including higher education differs considerably, both in quality and quantity, between students, as does the time span over which learning has taken place. The 'cultural capital' each graduate brings to the labour market varies accordingly. The extent to which higher education is able to compensate for earlier curricular gaps and shortcomings becomes an important issue for new categories of higher education entrants who do not originate from the traditional educational elite.

Under the general headings of 'transferable skills', 'competences' and 'enabling skills', the most common skills are seen to fall into three areas: communications skills (both oral and written), general intellectual problem-solving skills and numeracy; and social and interactive skills (Bradshaw, 1985). The HELM graduate panel surveys offer no opportunity for the assessment of skills development as such among graduates. Nor can the project offer evidence on employer evaluations of graduate abilities. There is, however, evidence to show that courses differ in the nature of skills qualifications students bring with them and that there have been changes in this regard. Further, the surveys give some insight into how graduates themselves perceive their work-related skills development, both as a result of higher education and through varieties of work experience and sandwich placements. Retrospective evaluations of the role of courses in fostering particular abilities are fraught with difficulties of interpretation, but they are also the closest higher education can get to a 'customer evaluation' of its activities and provisions.

Basic Skills and the Higher Education Curriculum

It is the task of schools to provide the initial development of basic skills. Much of the recent debate on the quality of schooling culminating in the Education Reform Act of 1988, which introduced a National Core Curriculum, has focused on both parental and employer demand for improved general standards of numeracy and literacy. Schools are being asked to monitor more publicly the training in such skills, and pupils are being asked to do a wider range of subjects and modes of assessment, as in for example the reformed GCSE system. Graduates in the HELM panel surveys passed through the education system in advance of such reforms, as mature students will continue to do for some time. However, in view of the perceived importance of the matter, it is still a worthwhile exercise to look at differences in background qualifications between subjects (with reference to such important pre-qualifications as O-level maths and English or their GCSE equivalents), to see whether any changes can be discerned between the 1982 and 1985 cohorts. The complex interaction between the size of student demand for places and formal course entry requirements would make it not unlikely that growth in student demand over the last ten years has led to an overall improvement in the background qualifications of students.

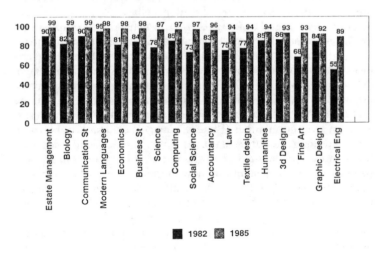

Figure 8.1: O-level English by course: comparing the 1982 and 1985 cohorts

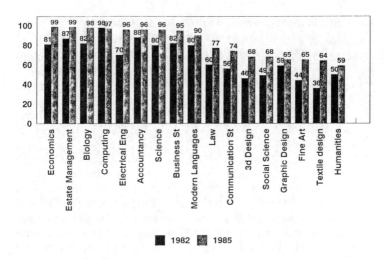

Figure 8.2: *O-level Maths by course: comparing the 1982 and 1985 cohorts*

There is an overall increase between the two cohorts in the proportions of students entering courses with O-level English. The most marked increase has been in electrical/electronic engineering and fine arts, but there have also been increases in social sciences, science and textile design (Figure 8.1.). There is a similar increase in the proportion of students entering the courses in our sample with O-level maths. There is a marked increase here for humanities, fine art, modern languages and social sciences (Figure 8.2.).

When it comes to basic background qualifications, 'more' in terms of expansion in student numbers has not meant 'worse'. Courses with higher proportions of non-standard entrants such as social sciences, humanities and communication studies show a considerable improvement in the proportions of students entering with O-level maths. With the demand for places in some subject areas remaining high, and a contraction of university provision in some areas, the competition for entry will continue to ensure that there is no threat to entry standards when it comes to the most basic educational qualifications. If, as has been suggested, one important dimension in the conception of 'employability' is that of a basic numeracy qualification, students in the 1985 cohort should be more 'employable'.

There are still, however, subject areas where the proportions with O-level maths fall short of 80 per cent: humanities (59%), textiles (65%), fine art (66%), graphic design (67%), 3D design (69%), social

Students, Courses and Jobs

sciences (70%), and law and communication studies (both 77%). These are also subject areas with higher proportions of mature and non-standard entrants, many of whom are women, and many of whom will have had neither the interest nor the opportunities to obtain relevant numeracy qualifications. These subject areas are also, as will be shown below, the ones where many students feel they have had insufficient opportunities to develop their numeracy during their studies. For students entering higher education without important background skills, does the experience of higher education offer compensations on the path towards becoming a competent graduate?

The Value and Benefits of the Higher Education Experience

The overall satisfaction experienced by graduates with the courses they take remains high for the 1985 sample, and confirms earlier evidence pointing to general student satisfaction with their higher education experience (Boys and Kirkland, 1988; Brennan and McGeevor, 1988). Overall, 89 percent of the graduates in the 1985 sample said, when asked to give their evaluation of the course, two years after graduation, that they were satisfied or very satisfied with their course although graduates from a handful of courses show some dissatisfaction (Figure 8.3.). The great majority (78%) of students would, if given the choice, do the same subject again (Figure 8.4.). It is important to note that courses with less than 80 per cent of gradu-

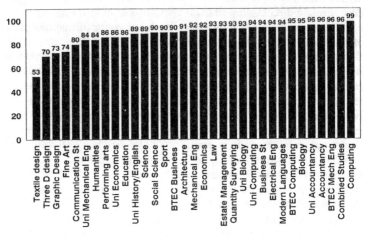

Figure 8.3: Evaluation of course as satisfied/very satisfied

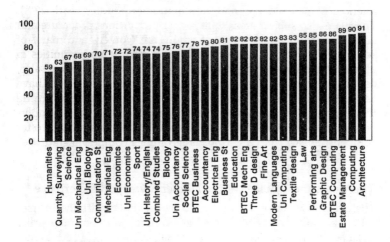

Figure 8.4: Would do the same course again

ates expressing a willingness to do the same subject again include not only those associated with a slower entry to employment, such as humanities and communication studies, but also, for example, quantity surveying, science and even economics, at both universities and polytechnics. As can be expected from the emphasis graduates put on personal interest in their choice of course to study, dissatisfactions do not relate directly to immediate employment prospects.

When asked whether the *content* of their degree course had been of real value to them in employment, 66 per cent of the 1985 sample thought their degree course had been useful and 69 per cent thought it would be in the future (Figures 8.5. and 8.6.). Courses such as humanities, fine arts, biology, communication studies and economics, where graduates expressed a feeling that so far their studies had been of less value to them in employment, are also courses where graduates show greater faith in its future value. This confirms evidence presented elsewhere about students' positive evaluations of the long term employment benefits that can be expected from higher education (Boys and Kirkland, 1988).

However, to be of analytical use such general questions need to be broken down into particular employment-related benefits. In a previous study it was shown that graduates from all subject areas considered that their time in higher education had some relevance to employment, but more in terms of the general critical and analytical skills gained than as a result of the specific academic knowledge of

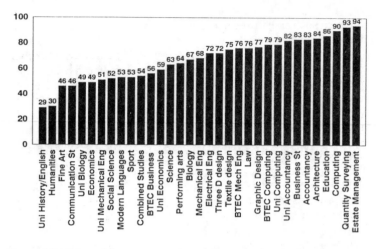

Figure 8.5: Value of degree course in employment: has been useful

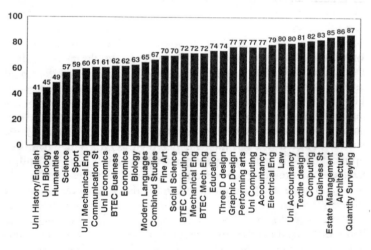

Figure 8.6: Value of degree course in employment: will be useful

the degree course itself (Boys and Kirkland, 1988). It may be that whereas many students choose a subject *content* primarily because of personal interest rather than its direct employment relevance, they see the *usefulness* to employment of their degree course lying in the opportunities offered to develop more personal and general kinds of skills. If that is the case, it becomes important to establish the extent to which such skills are perceived as improved by the higher education experience, no matter what the particular subject or course.

Both the 1982 and 1985 graduate panels were asked whether their experience of higher education had helped them improve in a range of employment-related abilities. The responses from the 1982 cohort have already been discussed in an earlier book (Brennan and McGeevor, 1988), but these results warrant further analysis in the light of the new evidence provided by students graduating from equivalent courses in 1985. The range of skills graduates of both cohorts were asked to consider covered most of the general skills and abilities referred to above, including general intellectual and personal abilities, such as critical thinking, independence, self-confidence, responsibility, leadership, as well as the basic skills of written and spoken communication and numeracy. The conclusion drawn by Brennan and McGeevor from the evidence of the 1982 cohort – that a considerable amount of consensus exists across most courses on many abilities – holds true for the 1985 cohort of graduates (Table 8.7.). Each respondent was asked to assess the extent of their benefits in terms of a four point scale: No Amount; A Small Amount; A Fair Amount; and A Great Amount. The scores given in Table 8.7. and subsequently are out of 100. A score of 33 and 36 correspond to the two middle categories. There is continued support for the contention that students see their degree courses as offering general intellectual as well as personal skills and abilities relevant to their employment, but not all courses in equal measure. There is also doubt expressed about the absence of some very basic skills benefits from courses in some subject areas. As for the 1982 cohort, general intellectual skills such as critical thinking, independence, organisation of work and the application of knowledge were perceived by most graduates in all subjects to have been considerably improved by higher education. Self-confidence and the understanding of other people are important further benefits. The rank ordering of benefits is virtually unaltered, with the general intellectual skills ranked highest and the same benefits tailing off at the lower end. But, as for the 1982 cohort, at the tail end of the list of perceived benefits there are greater variations between courses. The personal and social skills of spoken communication, co-operation, a sense of responsibility and leadership are all abilities required in graduate type careers, as is some level of numeracy. Yet students on many courses perceive that they had benefitted rather less as regards these latter skills.

To throw more light on the above, a table is presented showing a comparison between the evaluations of graduates from the equivalent courses in the two panels on a number of key abilities: the most and the least experienced benefits in the 1982 sample, critical thinking

Table 8.7: Do you consider that your experience in higher education helped you gain or improve any of the following abilities? (scores out of 100)

CNAA	CR	IN	OR	WR	APP	SE	UN	LO	SP	CO	RE	NU	PO	LE	NO
Accountancy	69	80	70	60	68	73	60	72	54	64	58	81	30	44	130
Architecture	83	79	75	51	74	68	63	70	66	67	64	37	30	54	103
Biology	73	81	78	67	75	66	59	68	50	65	54	67	30	38	174
Business Studies	77	78	73	69	66	70	61	68	65	63	52	68	35	52	129
Combined Studies	79	79	78	71	66	68	69	67	53	63	52	52	35	42	134
Communication Studies	87	73	66	77	66	65	66	50	60	59	46	16	29	34	81
Computing	64	74	72	49	70	63	53	80	48	60	51	61	28	37	145
Performing Arts	80	81	74	66	69	74	76	42	63	76	64	6	35	61	118
Estate Management	68	72	65	60	70	66	53	63	49	57	54	58	32	42	142
Economics	76	76	71	66	67	67	57	69	55	56	51	76	30	38	115
Education	73	74	73	66	69	75	69	53	65	65	63	29	32	69	131
Electrical Engineering	69	72	71	53	69	61	49	78	42	56	48	77	28	36	139
Fine Art	79	78	80	48	69	63	69	41	51	57	50	8	30	26	80
Graphic Design	81	78	74	47	65	61	65	55	47	61	54	11	31	40	97
Humanities	78	70	69	69	63	63	68	57	58	50	47	21	37	27	86
Law	82	70	66	68	78	64	58	71	55	47	46	9	33	32	105
Mechanical Engineering	75	76	74	63	70	68	54	77	50	61	53	81	30	43	127
Modern Languages	76	83	75	73	69	74	68	53	70	60	59	16	32	35	119
Quantity Surveying	68	67	72	61	68	63	48	66	46	55	53	70	33	44	100
Science	70	75	71	60	73	63	57	74	50	60	56	72	31	46	100

	CR	IN	OR	WR	APP	SE	UN	LO	SP	CO	RE	NU	PO	LE	NO
Social Science	80	63	64	72	68	63	71	59	57	49	42	49	29	32	112
Sport and Recreation	72	80	73	69	75	72	68	62	62	69	58	55	33	57	143
Textile and Fashion	73	82	79	43	70	66	62	50	48	59	59	19	28	38	108
3D Design	79	80	79	51	67	68	64	61	58	66	59	20	33	37	97
UNIVERSITY															
U Accountancy	73	88	70	56	67	73	70	69	47	56	52	75	30	41	95
U Biology	77	87	76	64	70	64	65	64	54	61	42	62	28	40	89
U Computing	70	73	72	41	74	64	55	87	38	56	48	74	32	38	93
U Economics	73	80	65	64	61	66	65	64	48	47	41	68	60	32	127
U History/English	85	82	74	78	68	68	70	54	65	52	50	10	56	35	285
U Mechanical Engineering	66	71	68	47	66	58	57	71	36	51	47	84	29	33	115
BTEC HIGHER NATIONAL															
BT Business	67	64	65	63	65	68	64	59	65	67	52	58	37	56	103
BT Computing	64	51	62	46	66	60	51	75	48	58	46	67	20	40	117
BT Mechanical Engineering	68	50	67	53	73	64	50	76	49	64	54	74	17	47	53
ALL COURSES	74	75	72	60	69	66	62	64	54	59	52	49	32	41	3892

CR = Critical thinking
WR = Written communication
UN = Understanding other people
CO = Cooperation with others
PO = Political awareness

IN = Independence
APP = Application of knowledge
LO = Logic
RE = Responsibility
LE = Leadership

OR = Organising own work
SE = Self-confidence
SP = Spoken communication
NU = Numeracy
NO = No of cases

Table 8.8: Benefits of higher education: cohort comparisons (scores out of 100)

	Critical Thinking	Written Communication	Spoken Communication	Numeracy	Leadership	All Benefits
Humanities						
82	85	80	65	19	30	55.8
85	78	69	58	21	27	50.6
(University English/History)	(85)	(78)	(65)	(10)	(35)	(54.6)
Modern Languages						
82	83	84	84	13	35	59.8
85	76	73	70	16	35	54.0
Communication Studies						
82	89	80	66	24	40	59.8
85	87	77	60	16	34	54.8
Accountancy						
82	71	63	50	75	28	57.4
85	69	60	54	81	44	61.6
(University Accountancy)	(73)	(56)	(47)	(75)	(41)	(58.4)
Business Studies						
82	73	64	52	73	39	60.2
85	77	69	65	68	52	66.2
Economics						
82	77	66	56	65	36	60.0
85	76	66	55	76	38	62.2
(University Economics)	(73)	(64)	(48)	(68)	(32)	(57.0)

	Critical Thinking	Written Communication	Spoken Communication	Numeracy	Leadership	All Benefits
Law						
82	82	67	59	7	32	49.4
85	82	68	55	9	32	49.2
Social Studies						
82	87	81	69	52	39	65.6
85	80	72	57	49	32	58.0
Electrical Engineering						
82	76	61	48	63	40	57.6
85	69	53	42	77	36	55.4
Computer Science						
82	73	58	51	59	40	56.2
85	64	49	48	61	37	51.2
	(70)	(41)	(38)	(74)	(38)	(52.2)
All courses						
82	80	70	60	47	36	58.6
85	76	66	56	47	34	55.8
(University Courses)	(75)	(60)	(50)	(57)	(37)	(55.8)

and leadership, as well as the three core skills of written and spoken communication and numeracy (Table 8.8.). As can be seen, graduates from the two cohorts come, on the whole, to very similar conclusions about the benefits they have received from their courses. The university courses included in the 1985 survey are put in brackets for comparisons. They can be seen to follow the same pattern and rank ordering as those given by the CNAA graduates. This consistency across cohorts and institutions indicates the potential advantages of a questionnaire approach to student course evaluation.

There are a few important points to note about Table 8.8. First, there are no major overall improvements in the students' perceptions between the two cohorts. The only subject area showing some improvement in most benefits is that of business studies, an area which has experienced a great deal of course development and growth in student numbers over the last few years. Graduates in 1985 from accountancy courses also evaluate their gains in numeracy more highly than graduates in 1982. Again, this is a curriculum area of growth and development. Apart from these two subject areas, overall the students in the 1985 cohort are a little more critical. This does not mean that courses have become less able to offer good teaching, but may instead reflect increased expectations among students for such benefits. The debate over the last decade on the relevance of higher education to employment opportunities may have increased students' expectations of the benefits higher education ought to bring.

Turning now to the distribution across courses of individual benefits, these can be graphically represented in a way that clearly shows the difference between those skills fostered as part of the higher education experience itself, irrespective of subject followed, and those which relate more closely to particular subject areas. Looking at the five benefits discussed above – critical thinking, written and spoken communication, numeracy and leadership – we can see the different profiles of distribution across courses of each benefit (Figures 8.9. to 8.13.). Most students on all courses see themselves as gaining a great deal in the development of their capacity for critical thinking. For gains in both written and spoken communication, differences begin to appear for a few courses, such as in the case of computing, fine arts, graphic design, textile and 3D design which do not score very well on written communication; and in the case of engineering subjects and quantity surveying which are poor performers on the benefit of oral communication. The position of numeracy stands out in all the charts. It is the one skill with the greatest fluctuation across courses in both samples, and the one that least fits the pattern of a 'general ability' improved by the higher education experience itself. The extent of the differences between subjects can be seen from Figure 8.12. where several subjects show very high scores and others extremely low ones. The argument for numeracy as a transferable skill across all graduate occupations in this age of technology and information processing has a long way to go before it is taken for granted across higher education curricula. As students with academically weaker, and older, secondary school qualifications are more likely to enter courses with fewer learning opportunities in numeracy and computing, it could be argued that the students most in need of these marketable skills get the least opportunity to develop them.

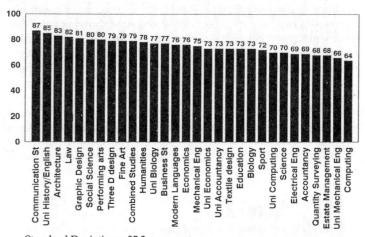

Standard Deviation = 25.2

Figure 8.9: Benefits of higher education: critical thinking

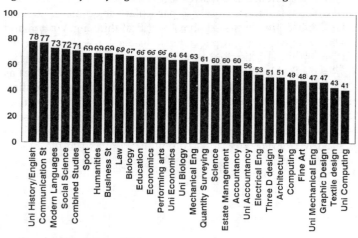

Standard Deviation = 28.6

Figure 8.10: Benefits of higher education: written communication

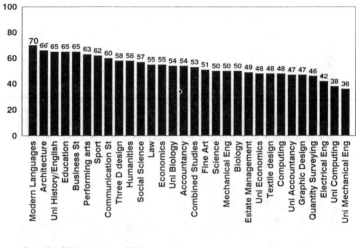

Standard Deviation = 29.0

Figure 8.11: Benefits of higher education: spoken communication

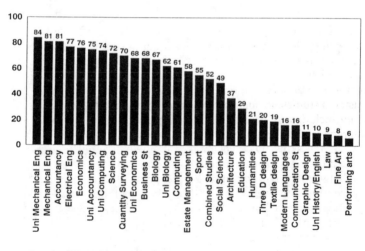

Standard Deviation = 37.3

Figure 8.12: Benefits of higher education: numeracy

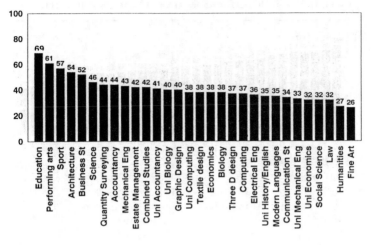

Standard Deviation = 30.0

Figure 8.13:Benefits of higher education: leadership

Lowest on the list of perceived benefits overall comes the skill of leadership. Only a few subject fields seem to have offered development in this area. These are notably the courses where some interactive 'role' skills are part of regular curricular practice, as in performing arts, education, sports and recreation, architecture and business studies. In such subject areas, interactive role exercises are often included as part of the learning programme. As social and interactive skills are one important aspect of what are seen to be transferable skills, this is yet another ability that cannot be seen to be 'picked up along the way' through studying for a degree. A comparison between the two cohorts as regards the performance of different subject areas on the three pertinent skills included in the survey question, points to the vocational nature of the subjects where graduates feel such skills have been fostered (Table 8.14.).

The evidence discussed throws some doubt on the idea that most courses in higher education provide the needed range of skills through a 'happy coincidence' between the teaching methods, assessment modes and research demands of an individual discipline and the skills demanded by employers (Lyon, 1988). Such an approach may work well for some of the general intellectual skills discussed above. There are, however, some kinds of skills which, unless positively identified and defined as relating to the work roles envisaged

Table 8.14: Role performance related benefits: top scorers

(a) Leadership

1982 Panel	*1985 Panel*
Nursing	Education
Hotel/Catering	Performing Arts
Production Engineering	Sport/Recreation
Environmental Planning	Architecture
Civil Engineering	Business Studies

(b) Co-operation

1982 Panel	*1985 Panel*
Nursing	Performing Arts
Environmental Planning	Sports/Recreation
Hotel/Catering	Architecture
Pharmacy	3D Design
Applied Biology	Biology

(c) Responsibility

1982 Panel	*1985 Panel*
Pharmacy	Architecture
Nursing	Performing Arts
Applied Chemistry	Education
Textiles/Fashion	3D Design
3D Design	Textiles/Fashion

for particular graduates, do not appear to be learned as a byproduct of good teaching and learning practice in individual disciplines.

Evaluating one's learning experience is not the same as expressing what one would like to have had more of. The panels of both 1982 and 1985 were asked whether their higher education experience had offered them sufficient or insufficient opportunities to develop some basic skills. The dissatisfactions expressed by the 1982 panel remain in 1985, as can be seen from the comparative Table 8.15., which shows the key skills previously reported as missing from some courses. Students in 'numerate' subjects such as accountancy, biology, computing, economics, electrical engineering and science continue in sizeable numbers to report that they had been given insufficient opportunities to develop their skills in oral communication. Regarding numeracy skills, the 1985 graduates from courses in communication studies, graphic design, law, humanities, social sciences, modern

Table 8.15: The extent to which graduates feel they have had opportunities to develop transferable skills (after two years) (1982 and 1985 panels)

Subject Field	Insufficient Opportunities Oral Communication		Insufficient Opportunities Numeracy		Insufficient Opportunities Computing	
	1982	1985	1982	1985	1982	1985
Accountancy	47.1	46.3	2.9	6.4	27.4	47.1
Business Studies	45.1	16.3	9.7	10.8	49.5	63.9
Biology	39.2	40.6	18.6	20.6	55.6	43.8
Communication Studies	8.6	15.9	47.4	52.5	49.2	52.6
Computing	39.0	43.9	7.3	15.0	0.9	2.4
Economics	37.5	43.5	18.8	11.9	44.6	58.1
Electrical/Electronic Engineering	53.8	60.7	0.0	6.6	4.1	28.6
Estate/Urban Management	40.0	31.4	17.8	22.9	51.0	55.6
Fine Art	25.0	16.9	15.8	23.2	26.8	13.2
Graphic Design	34.5	22.7	43.6	43.9	40.9	44.6
Humanities	15.2	6.6	36.4	38.2	47.3	41.8
Law	25.8	21.1	48.4	39.4	37.7	32.3
Modern Languages	8.3	9.3	47.5	36.5	49.0	48.3
Science	44.3	42.3	6.3	12.8	39.0	41.7
Social Studies	29.3	32.1	27.8	33.8	40.0	43.0
Textiles	31.4	25.8	41.5	33.8	42.9	29.3
3D Design			47.1	49.2	58.7	45.1

languages and textiles report in similar numbers to those graduating in 1982 that they had been given insufficient opportunities to develop this skill further. It is interesting to note that demands for computing skills are not being entirely met in 'numerate' courses such as accountancy, business studies, economics and electrical engineering, with a larger proportion of 1985 graduates in these areas reporting that they had been given insufficient opportunities to develop such skills.

It seems that, despite a small basic improvement in background qualifications, students often see themselves in need of more numeracy, especially on courses with higher proportions of students lacking maths O-level or equivalent qualifications and with slower patterns of entry to the labour market. Looking at the skill of computing, the 'demand' for more skills teaching can be seen to have gone *up* on courses which could already be expected to offer this skill as part of the discipline curriculum itself. These are areas where 'keeping up' with changes in knowledge and technology has and will pose both educational and resource problems for course planners. As the anticipated educational improvements from the recent Educational Reform Act will take some time to filter through into higher education, and as they will not directly affect mature and non-standard entrants, the issue of 'basic skills' will continue to be of some significance for higher education.

The Benefits of Work Experience

One way of 'bridging' the world of higher education and the world of work is to introduce students to some form of work experience as part of their course. Sandwich and other kinds of placements are designed to offer students an experience of the 'real' work place and to present them with an opportunity to draw together theory and practice. For professional education courses, such as nursing and education, the development of professional competence is seen as constituting a significant part of the course, with close co-operation between clinical and academically based teachers in teaching and assessment. The degree of integration between work experience and the academic components of the course varies between disciplines and professions, and the amount of 'experiential' learning that takes place clearly depends on the quality of the experience provided (DES, 1985). Work experience may serve students on two fronts in their relationship to the labour market: that of providing occupationally specific knowledge about the relationship between theory and practice in 'real' situations; and that of giving broader insights about the work place and how to manage effectively within it.

It is beyond the scope of this chapter to go into the details of the role of placements in teaching and learning in different subject areas. Nor is it an easy task to evaluate the cost effectiveness of such placements and the role of work experience in facilitating the process of finding employment. The ambivalence of employers to such schemes and the lack of detailed research in this area has been noted (Curwen, 1986). It is quite possible that those who choose to join courses with work placements of various kinds share further characteristics which facilitate success in the labour market. What the HELM surveys can tell us something about is students' perceptions of the benefits of work experience, sandwich placement being only one possibility, as part of a course of study, and whether the general satisfaction with such a course provision (see Boys *et al.* 1988) applies to the 1982 and 1985 cohorts of students. A comparison between equivalent courses among the two survey panels allows us to evaluate the consistency over time of student attitudes to their work experience.

There is little doubt that students who have had a period of work experience lasting more than 14 days as part of their courses feel positive towards that experience (see Table 8.16.).

Students who have had the opportunity to do a period of work experience are satisfied and glad they did. This is true across all subject areas offering such experience, and for all graduates in both panels. There is indication of some improvement in the evaluation by students on courses in 3D design and electrical/electronic engineering. Students without work experience on the whole wish they had had it. The proportion of students on courses without a work experience component who expressed a wish that they had been offered such experience never goes below around 50 per cent. The 'latent demand' from students in non-vocational subject areas for some form of work experience, observed in other recent surveys, can be discerned here also (Boys, *et al.* 1988). Overall, there is a marginally greater desire for work experience expressed by the 1985 panel, with graduates from courses in some subject areas showing considerable retrospective demand – biology, communication studies, graphic design, science and textile design. These are vocationally-related subject areas which, however, lack a clearly defined vocational outcome. They are also courses where, as has earlier been show, the graduates experience some difficulties in finding employment.

It may be, as Boys and Kirkland note with regard to their similar findings, that vocational elements in courses are used to provide some compensation both for low entry qualifications and the lower

Table 8.16: Evaluation of work experience (WEX) 1982 and 1985 panels (%)

Subject Field	1982 Proportion With WEX Who Are Satisfied	1982 Proportion Without WEX Who Wish Had	1985 Proportion With WEX Who Are Satisfied	1985 Proportion Without WEX Who Wish Had
Accountancy	100.0	61.8	100.0	62.5
Business Studies	85.9	All WEX	99.5	All WEX
Biology	90.7	77.3	100.0	75.0
Communication Studies	No WEX	72.4	No WEX	77.3
Computer Science	90.2	All WEX	99.8	All WEX
Economics	No WEX	54.8	No WEX	65.5
Electrical/Electronic Engineering	74.2	50.0	96.4	68.9
Estate/Urban Management	93.3	76.9	100.0	60.7
Fine Art	No WEX	48.7	No WEX	55.7
Graphic Design	92.3	88.2	96.6	92.7
Humanities	100.0	30.4	No WEX	59.2
Law	No WEX	48.4	No WEX	57.0
Modern Languages	100.0	49.1	100.0	57.7
Science	97.2	58.2	100.0	71.4
Social Science	No WEX	51.9	100.0	52.0
Textile Design	80.0	89.7	100.0	88.6
3D Design	75.0	78.0	90.0	78.0

attraction to employers of graduates from public sector institutions (Boys and Kirkland, 1988).

To gain some insight into the particular benefits students perceive they gain from work experience, a more detailed analysis of course types in the 1985 cohort has been carried out (Figures 8.17. to 8.24.). For the panel as a whole, the main benefits are seen to lie in the development of the more general personal skills discussed above: communication skills, personal confidence and general problem solving. The gains in these personal skills are seen as important by students in most subject areas, although less so for courses in electrical/electronic engineering, quantity surveying, textile and graphic design. These are course types where students may be more likely to enter the work place as technical assistants at a lower level and with less demands on personal interactions, rather than as full blown participants in the work situation at hand, compared with for example education, languages, business studies and the performing arts. When it comes to problem-solving, however, some of the more technologically-orientated course types do better. The potential benefit of increased commercial awareness is very unevenly spread across courses, and here we come again to a skill which appears to be more specifically related to the type of employment at which a course is aimed. It does not appear to be a more generally shared benefit of work experience itself. The same is the case for numeracy and leadership skills, which on the whole are only seen as of major benefit on a few courses. Except on the vocationally associated courses of the performing arts, education, architecture, sports and 3D design, students are less favourable in their evaluation of the role of work experience relative to its contribution to course work. Lack of integration between the work placement and academic parts of a particular course has been a frequently raised criticism of the value of work experience, a view shared by some students in the HELM surveys.

There is a great difference between students from different subject areas in the way they perceive the employment-related value of their period of work experience (see Figure 8.25.). Although all students feel benefits have been gained, this is less so for social science and accountancy students than for performing arts, textile design, architecture and biology students. Each subject area needs to be surveyed in greater detail to get closer to the kinds of benefits and skills which work experience can offer students in a particular subject or a particular course. The very positive evaluation of work experience offered by students overall, whatever the subject area of study, and the kinds of *general* personal skills students feel they gain from that experience, makes us believe that closer attention to work experience on courses in higher education is warranted *irrespective* of whether it

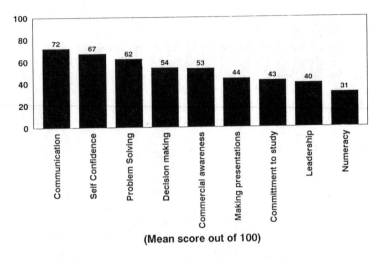

Figure 8.17: Work experience benefits: all students 1985

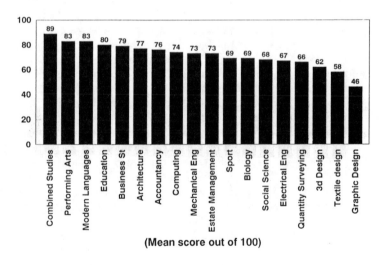

Figure 8.18: Work experience benefits (1985 panel): helped
communication

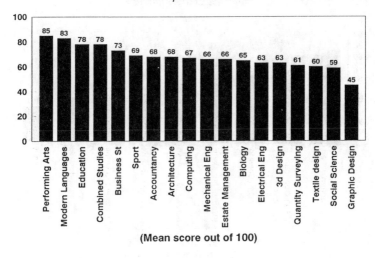

*Figure 8.19: Work experience benefits (1985 panel): helped
self-confidence*

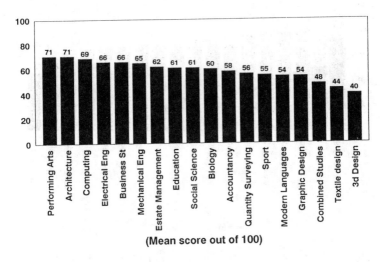

*Figure 8.20: Work experience benefits (1985 panel): helped problem
solving*

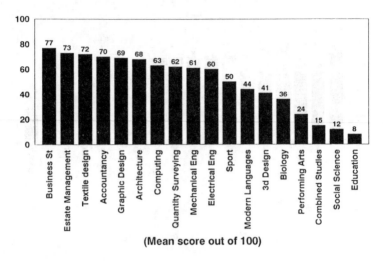

Figure 8.21: Work experience benefits (1985 panel): helped commercial awareness

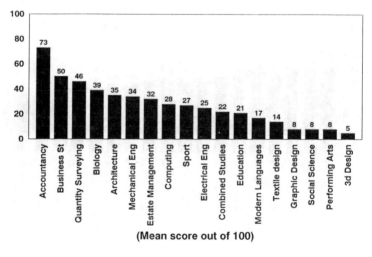

Figure 8.22: Work experience benefits (1985 panel): helped numeracy

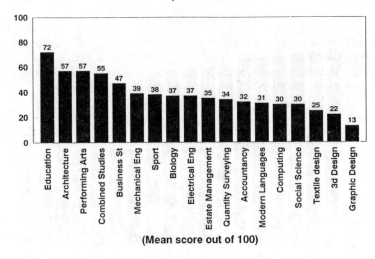

Figure 8.23: Work experience benefits (1985 panel): helped leadership

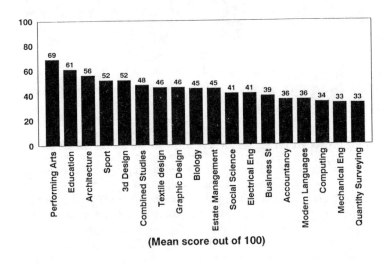

*Figure 8.24: Work experience benefits (1985 panel): helped
    commitment to course work*

Students, Courses and Jobs

facilitates finding employment. In view of the emphasis placed by both students and employers on the development of transferable personal skills, the rationale and justification for including a period of work experience on courses may lie as much in this general area as in the preparation of particular and specific vocational skills.

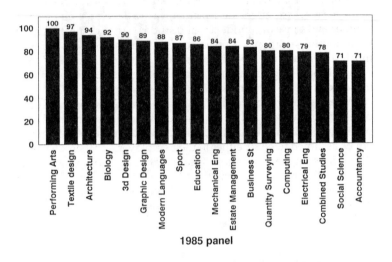

Figure 8.25: Work experience and job prospects: proportion receiving benefits

A Personally Competent Graduate

There is ample evidence that neither students nor their teachers (through whose courses students pass on their way to a degree) wish to see higher education solely as a training ground for industry and the economy. Students in search of specific and well defined vocational specialisms find these on varieties of tightly defined professional courses. Other students may not have a job or a career in mind when they enter higher education, and are still searching while pursuing varieties of temporary employment and post-graduate studies. Underneath these differences in the strength of occupational and career orientations, a common theme may begin to emerge – a theme which appears to be shared by both graduates and employers. This is the belief that one of the key aims of higher education is that of fostering the development of a more general spectrum of skills and abilities. Students feel positive towards their higher education experience and the cultural and analytical skills it brings. They are, however, less certain about a range of particular skills which, unless positively articulated as part of the curriculum of their chosen discipline, do not develop themselves. When such skills are missing from the social and educational background of students as well as from a particular curriculum, their absence stands out as more acute. Students see work experience as a further way to develop their personal abilities and sense of confidence, and students who do not receive it, even on non-vocational courses, tend to want some. This is not so much a demand for 'vocationalism' or 'industrial relevance', as a demand for a greater emphasis on a broader general education in those skills areas which make for a 'competent' person.

Whereas generations of arts graduates from the ancient universities have been assumed to be competent on the strength of their privileged social and educational background, graduates today cannot be assumed to be so, either in their employers' or their own eyes. With 'mass' higher education close at hand, there may be grounds not only for the continuation of the debate on broadening the nature of secondary school qualifications, but also for the widening of the undergraduate curriculum in order to give students a more genuinely general education for competence.

Chapter Nine

Conclusions and Policy Implications

A Changing Context

Two general trends are discernable in the employment demand for graduates in the 1990s, notwithstanding labour market fluctuations. The first is the steady increase in the numbers of jobs with a high knowledge and skills base and which require graduate level education. The second trend, arising from the rapidity of technological development and consequent changes in the organisation of work, is in the demand for new kinds of skills – notably in information technology but also in many other areas, for example languages. With this has come the recognition that rapidity of change will require continuing professional education throughout a working life.

There has always been debate about how well higher education has prepared its graduates for employment. The debate has ranged across not only arts-based subjects – where relevance has been questioned – but has included vocational education in areas as diverse as engineering and education. Educators have increasingly accepted the imperative to be 'useful' and 'relevant', sometimes prompted by government departments bearing money and sometimes, particularly in the polytechnics in recent years, out of an institutional embrace of a 'vocational' and 'service' mission. Thus, in the last decade a wealth of curriculum developments have steered higher education towards a greater concern with qualities of 'enterprise', 'competence' and 'capability' and with the IT and other skills necessary to achieve them.

The expansion of higher education during the 1980s led to the entry of ever wider sections of the population. Institutions have found themselves teaching students from a wider range of social and educational backgrounds and with expectations and ambitions different from those of their traditional clients. Increasingly, higher education has been teaching different things to different kinds of people. In so doing, has it been serving society, and more particularly the labour market, better or worse? How has it been serving its students?

The relationship between higher education and the labour market has been explored in this book through the analysis and discussion of data collected from graduates throughout the 1980s and into the 1990s. All of the graduates in our samples had completed their studies by the middle of the decade. Thus, our study could not examine the impact of more recent initiatives, such as the Department of Employment Enterprise in Higher Education programme, although such initiatives are substantially foreshadowed by earlier educational developments in the polytechnics, from which the largest proportions of our samples were drawn. The demand for new graduates fluctuated during the decade with our 1982 cohort catching a trough and our 1985 cohort enjoying a peak. But our follow-up of both cohorts enabled us to draw conclusions about the 'helm' relationship on firmer evidence than that provided by statistics on initial entry to employment.

Continuity and Change

Notwithstanding periodic media scares, our studies revealed no serious long-term unemployment among graduates. The state of the labour market undoubtedly influences the ease and speed of entry into employment but, for both cohorts, most graduates had succeeded in finding permanent employment within two years of graduation. The relative advantage of different subjects was also largely independent of labour market fluctuations with continued evidence that students from the less vocational courses take longer to obtain jobs and receive lower rates of pay. Levels of job satisfaction, however, do not relate closely to objective indicators of employment success.

It has been one of the main arguments of this book that to regard relative employability of different types of graduate as simply a reflection of employer preferences would be mistaken. Students look for many things from their higher education and graduates seek many things from employment. The recruitment of graduates reflects the preferences of the graduates as well as the preferences of employers. The relationship between student values and the subject(s) studied is a reminder that the 'helm' relationship is not a mechanistic one but is formed out of the socially and culturally contextualised decisions of many thousands of individuals, each pursuing personal goals, each reflecting personal orientations to work and to life. As higher education extends its accessibility to wider sections of society, the range of student orientations can be expected to broaden. This will have implications for the kinds of places which higher education institutions are going to become and for the types of relationship to be forged with the labour market in future.

Although the study focused on the employment experiences of graduates from the rapidly expanding polytechnic and college sector (the larger of the two sectors by the end of the decade), comparison with university graduates confirmed the evidence of first destinations data that university graduates hold a distinct advantage in the labour market. Not only do university graduates obtain jobs more quickly, they receive better rates of pay and they obtain more rapid promotion. After a few years, university graduates are more likely to have moved into managerial positions. They are also more likely initially to go into finance or 'fast track' management, irrespective of the subject studied. These points may justify the less vocational nature of many university courses. Their graduates may spend less time than their polytechnic and college counterparts in jobs which use specific vocational skills acquired as an undergraduate.

As we have noted, institutions differ in important respects in terms of the 'social catchment' of their students. It is these input differences which appear to be substantially responsible for the differences in employment profiles of their graduate outputs. For this reason, it seems unlikely that the change in title of polytechnics to universities will have much effect on existing graduate employment differences unless via an effect on the student recruitment to these institutions. However, the mediating effect of degree class should also be noted. For many subjects, class of degree appears to be more important than institution attended: better a 2:1 from a polytechnic than a 2:2 from a university.

The influence of institutional differences is but one aspect of the structural inequalities which underpin the 'helm' relationship. As we have emphasised throughout this report, graduates enjoy radically different employment prospects according to the subject of their degree course as well as the institution attended. Employment prospects, as our own and other reports repeatedly demonstrate, differ for graduates according to their gender, their social class and their ethnic origins. These factors appear to have both a direct effect on employment and an indirect one via their relationship to the intervening factors of subject studied and institution attended. This interactive relationship raises old questions about how far the education system is a sorting device for social and economic stratification or a source of legitimation of inequalities whose origins lie elsewhere in society. However, to focus on this question may be to miss the significance and scale of the benefits graduates acquire from their higher education.

If there remain general inequalities of outcome which favour students from socially advantaged backgrounds attending traditional universities, there are personal 'inequalities' of benefit which favour socially disadvantaged students attending the inner-city polytechnics. Whereas the former have an already advantaged social and economic position confirmed by higher education, for the latter higher education provides a passport out of underprivileged and new opportunities for social and economic advance. In terms of value added to the individual, a comparatively modest employment success may represent personal achievements of life-transforming potential.

The 'helm' relationship

Within the framework of the model presented in Chapter Three and in line with the target areas for analysis outlined in Chapter One, the project evidence points to a few key issues of policy concern with implications for both students, institutions and employers.

1. There is continued evidence of a relationship between on the one hand *student orientations* and student social and educational background, and on the other between student orientations and choice of course. Students from 'less favoured' social and educational backgrounds show less evidence of well defined career orientations and choose courses with less direct links with the labour market. This is partly because in a competitive higher education market there is a clear ranking between subjects, as well as institutions, in the kinds of educational entry qualifications demanded. The 'new' recruits into an expanding higher education may increasingly have to look towards vocationally-oriented Masters courses to improve their labour market position. On the other hand, students with well defined career orientations choosing vocational courses and subjects several years before entering the labour market, may well have seen their aspirations frustrated if the demand for their specialist skills is low at the time they graduate, unless they come from more 'favoured' social and educational backgrounds with a wider range of desirable credentials than a degree alone.

2. In their position as a mediating stage between student demand for higher education and demands in the economy for graduate labour, *subjects and courses* occupy a strong position. Independent of labour market conditions, labour market success depends on a combination of subject undertaken and personal characteristics. What we have termed vocationally specific courses show the best

employment patterns overall. However, given the varied labour market orientations of students, this leaves institutions in a somewhat contradictory position. Should the value of a course be assessed by the numbers of students it is able to attract, especially desired 'new' recruits amongst women and mature students, or by the speed of entry to the labour market of its graduates? Our evidence points to the fact that courses high on one of these measures may fall on the other. In a period of expansion, this will inevitably leave institutions in some difficulty when it comes to interpreting the social and economic 'responsiveness' of higher education. 'Mass' higher education may not lead to a greater 'fit' between course provisions and specific labour market demand, but instead to an increase in the general educational level of labour market recruits. With, as our data shows, many graduate jobs recruiting from a very wide variety of subject backgrounds, the labour market as a whole will continue to absorb graduates. This may mean, however, that employers will themselves increasingly have to become involved in specialist vocational training tailored to their own specific, often temporary, demands and higher education institutions will need to devote more of their resources to continuing professional education.

3. There is only limited evidence that students respond in any immediate sense to changes in *labour market demands*. We found some evidence that the students in the 1985 cohort had tended to revise downwardly their employment aspirations in the short-term, possibly in response to the publicity given to graduate unemployment in the preceding years. However, two years after graduation there is little difference in employment status between students graduating in the same subjects in the 1982 and 1985 cohorts, despite differences in labour market opportunities. The difference lies more in the nature of recruiting organisations, with better labour market conditions allowing a higher proportion of graduates amongst both men and women, to enter larger firms in the private sector, and a declining proportion employed in the public sector, especially for men. Our evidence clearly illustrates the gender-segmented nature of the graduate labour market. As has been shown elsewhere, proclaimed skills shortages and higher salaries in some areas, notably technology, engineering and commerce, do not seem to have led to any major increases in either mature or women students choosing to study subjects in these areas in higher education as a whole, except perhaps commerce. Women

in our panels attracted to jobs in these areas do well, though not as well as their fellow male graduates, but this may be partly for the simple reason that there are still so few of them. The different position in the graduate labour market occupied by women is well illustrated by the marked differences in the effect of family formation on male and female employment status. Bringing women into traditionally male sectors of the graduate labour market will require a great deal more than increasing the number of women into male domains of higher education.

4. The strength of patterns of stratification between types of *higher education* institutions have yet again been documented here. Although subject chosen remains the more important factor when it comes to patterns of entry to the labour market, for some subjects the nature of the institution attended becomes an important variable to take into consideration. The labour market relationship of, for example, graduates from humanities courses in universities is very different from that of polytechnic graduates in the same area. The differences in employment outcomes are not as great on more vocationally specific courses, such as computing, with graduates in high demand in the labour market. Whether this is due to the lower status of polytechnics in the eyes of employers, or to the different nature of the student body, cannot be ascertained in this report. It is still the case that the actual process by which recruitment decisions are made by employers is as much of a 'black box' in need of further investigation as the process by which students get recruited to courses.

5. In view of the fact that higher education has to serve a growing potential student market as well as a labour market, *student evaluation* of courses and their usefulness becomes as important for institutions as employer evaluations of graduates as 'products'. In both panels of the HELM survey, graduates have expressed important views about the employment relevance of their chosen subject of study. The evidence shows the graduates to have a more complex and sophisticated view of 'relevance' than that measured by success in getting a job. The emphasis of graduates on personal interest as an objective in seeking higher education on the whole appears to be satisfied. Satisfaction with course of study does not relate to the immediate employment prospects of the subject studied. But when it comes to more specific employment-related skills students do continue to express criticisms, and there is evidence that general personal skills, unless positively identified in the curriculum, do not

appear to be satisfactorily dealt with in many subject areas. The remarkable similarity between the views of the 1982 and 1985 graduates in this respect suggests that curriculum developments during this period were not keeping pace with the changing demands of work. That such skills are seen as part of general personal development rather than an expression of specific vocational need, is reinforced by student evaluation of work experience as a positive contribution towards the development of general personal skills. Evidence from the HELM panel strongly points towards the existence of a demand amongst graduates themselves for a greater emphasis on a broader general education in those skills areas which can be seen to make for a 'competent person'.

A New Higher Education

The changes foreshadowed in the 1991 White Paper will be the most fundamental for higher education in Britain since the Robbins expansion of the 1960s. Expansion and diversity, at the very least, draw larger sections of both society and the labour market into the 'helm' relationship. Too many current debates about graduate employment centre on a 'milk round' view of the relationship which is relevant to only a proportion of graduates and graduate employers. That proportion will continue to decrease as expansion continues. Just as students will come from ever broader sections of society, so too will graduates enter new areas of the labour market. Higher education will become much less of an initial sorting process into pre-set labour market slots. The slots themselves are continually changing. Most people can expect to have several careers rather than one. Earlier in this book we noted how far many graduates had moved from original vocational specialisms in even the first three years in the labour market. Indeed, the more successful the graduate, the further the distance that is likely to have been travelled from any specialist skills inculcated by a first degree.

The transformative potential of these trends should not be underestimated. Teichler *et al.* (1980) have described how the nature of an occupation changes in response to changes in the educational level of its labour force. The 'helm' relationship is never static. The mismatch between what higher education produces and what the labour market requires at a given time may, rather than being a problem, in fact be a major creative force. When seeking to respond to the needs of employers, higher education institutions should not forget that their graduates of today are the employers of tomorrow.

Bibliography

Acker, S. and Warren Piper, D. (eds) (1984) *Is Higher Education Fair to Women?* Guildford: SHRE/NFER-Nelson.

Ball, C. (1989) *Aim Higher: Widening Access to Higher Education* (Interim Report for the Education/Industry Forum's Higher Education Steering Group). London: RSA/Industry Matters.

Bosworth, D. and Ford, J. (1985) 'Perceptions of higher education by university entrants: an exploratory study'. *Studies in Higher Education* Vol. 10, No. 3.

Boys, C., Brennan, J., Henkel, M., Kirkland, J., Kogan, M. and Youll, P. (1988) *Higher Education and the Preparation for Work*. London: Jessica Kingsley Publishers.

Boys, C. and Kirkland, J. (1988) *Degrees of Success*. London: Jessica Kingsley Publishers.

Bradshaw, D. (1985) 'Transferable intellectual and personal skills'. *Oxford Review of Education* Vol. 11, No. 2.

Brennan, J. and McGeevor, P. (1988) *Graduates at Work*. London: Jessica Kingsley Publishers.

Brennan, J. and McGeevor, P. (1990) *Ethnic Minorities and the Graduate Labour Market*. London: CRE.

Craigh, S. *et al.* (1986) 'Self-employment in Britain: Results from the Labour Force Surveys 1981–1984'. *Employment Gazette*, June, No. 6.

Craigh, S. and Rees, A. (1989) 'Graduates in the labour market in the 1980s: Result from the Labour Force Survey'. *Employment Gazette*, January, No. 1.

Curwen, P. (1986) 'Another bite of the sandwich'. *THES* 19 November.

DES (1985) *An assessment of the Costs and Benefits of Sandwich Education*. (The RISE Report).

DES (1987) *Higher Education: Meeting the Challenge*, CM 114. London: HMSO.

DES (1990) *Highly Qualified People: Supply and Demand*. (Report of an Interdepartmental Review) London: HMSO.

Dippelhofer-Stien, B. *et al.* (1984) 'Students in Europe: Motives for studying, expectations of higher education and the relevance of career prospects'. *European Journal of Education*, Vol. 19, No. 3.

Employment Gazette (1988) 'Labour force outlook to 1995', March, No. 3.

Employment Gazette (1989) 'Labour force outlook to the year 2000', April, No. 4.

Fleming, A. (1988) 'Employment in the public sector 1982–1988'. *Employment Trends*, No. 422, December.

Fulton, O. (1988) 'Elite survivals? Entry 'standards' and procedures for higher education admissions'. *Studies in Higher Education*, Vol. 13, No. 1.

Gatley, D. (1988) *The Influence of Social Class Origins on the Choice of Course, Career Preferences and entry to Employment of CNAA Graduates*, PhD thesis, Staffordshire Polytechnic.

Institute of Manpower Studies (1990) 'Access to higher education in the 1990s and beyond'. Brighton: IMS Working Paper 155.

Lyon, E.S. and Gatley, D. (1988) *Black Graduates and Labour Market Recruitment.* London: HELM Working Paper 5, South Bank Polytechnic.

Lyon, E.S. (1988) *Academic Abilities and Transferable Skills: A Discussion.* London: HELM Working Paper 7, South Bank Polytechnic.

Lyon, E.S., McGeevor, P. and Murray, K. (1988) *After Higher Education: The Experience of a Sample of 1985 Graduates and Diplomates Two Years After Graduation.* London: HELM Publication, South Bank Polytechnic.

Lyon, E.S. and Murray, K. (1993) 'Graduate labour markets and the new vocationalism in higher education'. In G. Payne and M. Cross (eds) *Sociology in Action.* London: Macmillan.

Meadows, P. and Cox, R. (1987) 'Employment of graduates, 1975–1990'. *Employment Gazette,* April, No. 4.

Morgan, W.J. and Scott, N.T. (1987) *Unemployed Graduates: A Wasted National Resource.* Nottingham: University of Nottingham, Centre of Labour and Management Studies.

National Advisory Board (1986) *Transferable Personal Skills in Employment: The Contribution of Higher Education.* London: NAB.

Pearson, R. (1976) *Qualified Manpower in Employment.* Brighton: Institute of Manpower Studies.

Pearson, R. and Rajan, A. (eds) (1986) *UK Occupational and Employment Trends to 1990.* London: Institute of Manpower Studies/Butterworths.

Pearson, R. and Pike, G. (1989) *The Graduate Labour Market in the 1990s.* Brighton: IMS Report No. 167, Institute of Manpower Studies.

Phillips, C. (1987) 'The mature graduate labour market'. *Employment Gazette,* June, No. 6.

Redpath, B. and Harvey, B. (1987) *Young People's Intention to Enter Higher Education.* OPCS. London: HMSO.

Roizen, J. and Jepson, M. (1985) *Degrees for Jobs: Employer Expectations of Higher Education.* Guildford: SRHE/NFER-Nelson.

Sanyal, B.C. (1987) *Higher Education and Employment.* London: The Falmer Press.

Scott, N. (1982) 'Graduate supply and demand in 1982'. *Employment Gazette,* February No. 2.

Silver, H. and Brennan, J. (1988) *A Liberal Vocationalism.* London: Methuen.

Tarsh, J. (1985) 'The labour market for new graduates in 1983'. *Employment Gazette,* May, No. 5.

Tarsh, J. (1986) 'The labour market for new graduates in 1984'. *Employment Gazette,* September, No. 9.

Tarsh, J. (1989) 'New graduate destinations by age of graduation'. *Employment Gazette,* November, No. 11.

Teichler, U., Harting, D. and Nuthmann, R. (1980) *Higher Education and the Needs of Society.* Windsor: NFER.

Thomas, K. (1990) *Gender and Subject in Higher Education.* Milton Keynes: Open University Press/SRHE.

Wilson, R.A., Bosworth, D.L. and Taylor, P.T. (1990) *Projecting the Labour Market for the Highly Qualified.* Coventry: Institute of Employment Research, University of Warwick.

Williams, G. (1989) 'Higher Education'. In M. Flude and M. Hammer (eds) *Education Reform Act 1988: Origins and Implications.* London: Falmer Press.

Subject Index

References in italic indicate figures or tables.

A-level results 29, 30, *31*, *32*
and job type *83*, 84
and institutional type *94*, *98*, 99
access to higher education 28–33, *31–2*
access courses 29
accountancy courses *see* subject areas: 1982 panel; subject areas: 1985 panel
accountancy employers *see* employing organisations
accountancy jobs *see* job types
acting jobs *see* job types
administrative jobs *see* job types
admission policies *see* entry requirements
advertising jobs *see* job types
age of students *see* mature students
agriculture courses 54
'altruistic' job orientation *36*, 37, *39*, *39*, *40*, 41
amenity management *see* job types
'application of knowledge' ability *118–19*
architecture courses *see* subject areas: 1985 panel
architecture employers *see* employing organisations
architecture jobs *see* job types
art and design jobs *see* job types
arts graduates 52, 53, 138
aspirations *see* student orientations
banking jobs *see* job types
banking employers *see* employing organisations
basic skills 128
higher education *see* transferable skills
pre-higher education 112–14, *112*, *113*
biology courses *see* subject areas: 1982 panel; subject areas: 1985 panel
broadcasting jobs *see* job types
BTEC awards 8, *14*, *16*, 99–108, *98*, *99*, *101*, *103*, *104*, *106*
business studies courses *see* subject areas: 1982 panel; subject areas: 1985 panel
Business and Technician Education Council *see* BTEC courses

career development 105–8, *106*
career progression 88–92
family formation 89–91, *89*, *90*
geographical mobility 91–2, *91*, *92*
salaries 88–9, *88*, *90*
career prospects, as study motivation *38*, 39
'careerist' job orientation 34–7, *35*, *39*, *39*, *40*
chemicals employers *100*
chemistry courses *13*, *17*, *35*, *36*, *126*
child-rearing, and career progression 89, 90, *89*, *90*, *91*, *92*
civil engineering courses *13*, *17*, *35*, *36*, *126*
civil engineering employment 64, 65, 87
civil service *see* employing organisations
clerical jobs *see* job types
CNAA awards 8, *13–14*, 99–108, *98*, *99*, *100–1*, *103*, *104*, *106*
cohort comparisons, research methods 20, *20*
combined studies courses *see* subject areas: 1985 panel
commercial awareness *132*, *134*
commercial employers *see* employing organisations
'commitment to study', as work experience benefit *132*, *135*
communication skills 111, 131, *132*
spoken 117, *118–19*, *120–1*, *122*, *124*, *126*, *127*
written 117, *118–19*, *120–1*, *122*, *123*
communication studies courses *see* subject areas: 1982 panel; subject areas: 1985 panel
competences, employment-related 109–37, 144
basic skills 112–14, *112*, *113*
higher education benefits 114–17, *114*, *115*
transferable skills *116*, 117–28, *118–19*, *120–1*, *123–5*, *126*, *127*
work experience benefits 128–36, *130*, *132–5*, *136*
computing courses *see* subject areas: 1982 panel; subject areas: 1985 panel
computing skills *127*

'co-operation with others' ability *118–19*, *126*
course types 58, 61–3, 70–3, 95, 139, *141–2*, 143
courses 2–3, 23–7, *26*, 55–6, *141–2*
see also course types; institution types; qualification types; subject areas
creative jobs *see* job types
creative courses *see* subject areas: 1985 panel
critical thinking skills *118–19*, *120–1*, *122*, *123*
CSE examination passes 42–3

decision making skills *132*
degree class 140
and job type *83*, 84
and salary *104*, 105
Department of Employment Enterprise in Higher Education programme 139
'discipline based' subjects 61, 62, 71, 72
'dual labour market' 48–9, 58

Early Destination Statistics *see* First Destination Statistics
economics courses *see* subject areas: 1982 panel; subject areas: 1985 panel
education courses *see* subject areas: 1985 panel
Education for Capability project 7
educational experience, previous 22, 75, 98–9, 112–14, 141
see also A-level results; O-level results; schools, fee-paying
electrical engineering courses *see* subject areas: 1982 panel; subject areas: 1985 panel
employing organisations 49, 50, 52–3, *64–5*, 66–8, *100–1*, 102
salaries offered *87*, *88*
size 68–70
Employment of Humanities Graduates project 7
employment-related competences *see* competences
employment status 67, 69, 142
course type 70–3
family formation and gender 89–90, *89*
see also full-time employment; full-time

study; part-time
employment;
unemployment
employment take-up rates
57–8, 58–9, 63, 66
employment trends 49–51
graduate 51–5, 138
segmentation 55–6
employment types *see* job types
enabling skills *see* transferable
skills
engineering consultants 87, 101
engineering design jobs *see* job
types
engineering employers *see*
employing organisations
engineering jobs *see* job types
engineering R & D jobs *see* job
types
English courses *see* subject
areas: 1982 panel
English O-level results 42, 98,
98, 112–13, 112
Enterprise Initiative 7, 110
entertainment employers 64
entry requirements, higher
education 29–30, 113, 141
environmental planning
courses 14, 17, 35, 36, 126
environmental science courses
14, 17, 35, 36
estate management courses *see*
subject areas: 1982 panel;
subject areas: 1985 panel
estate management jobs *see* job
types
ethnic minorities 6, 22, 140
examination results *see* A-level
results; degree class; O-level
results
'extrinsic' goals 33, 34

family background
course type 46, 46, 99, 100–2
job orientation 39, 40
job type 84, 85, 86
salaries 104–5, 104
family formation, and career
progression 89–92, 89, 90,
91, 92
fathers *see* family background
female graduates *see* gender
finance employers *see*
employing organisations
finance jobs *see* job types
fine art courses *see* subject
areas: 1982 panel; subject
areas: 1985 panel
First Destination Return (FDR)
4–6, 57
First Destination Statistics
(FDS) 3, 52, 54, 59, 95

food, drink and tobacco
employers 88
full-time employment 67, 69,
89, 90, 96
full-time study 67, 69, 70, 71,
72, 89, 90

gas, electricity and water employers 87
GCE *see* A-level results; O-level
results
gender 6, 22, 24, 41, 48–9, 50–1,
58, 140, 142–3
employing organisations
64–5, 68, 87
employment status 67, 69,
70–3
family formation 89–92, 89,
90, 91, 92
GCE passes 42–3
job orientation 39, 39
job types 74–5, 84, 85, 86
previous education 42–3
salaries 87, 88, 90, 90
subject choice 44, 61
general skills *see* transferable
skills
geographical mobility 91, 91, 92
geography courses 14, 17, 35, 36
government policy 6–7
graduate destinations 4–6,
57–73, 74–92
critical discussion 59–60
degree subject 60–3
employment status 67, 69,
70–3
gender, family formation
and career progression
88–92, 88, 89, 90, 91, 92
job recruitment profile
75–84, 76–80, 81–3
social background 84, 85–7
speed of entry 63, 66
see also employing
organisations
Graduate Model 61
'graduate orientations' 2, 3
graduate parents 84, 85, 86
graduate research samples
15–16, 15–16, 19–20,
response rate 17, 18–19
graduate 'shortages' 6, 10, 110
graduate type *see* educational
experience; family
background; gender; social
background
graphic design courses *see*
subject areas: 1982 panel;
subject areas: 1985 panel

health authority employment
see employing organisations

HELM (Higher Education and
the Labour Market) project
1–2, 9
'helm' relationship 1, 2, 4, 22–4,
141–4
model 25–8, 26
Higher Education for
Capability Project 110
Higher Education and the
Labour Market (HELM)
project 1–2, 9
History courses 31, 32
student evaluation 114, 115,
116, 119, 123, 124, 125
hotel and catering courses 14,
17, 35, 36, 126
hotel and catering employers
see employing organisations
'human capital approach' 6–7
humanities courses *see* subject
areas: 1982 panel; subject
areas: 1985 panel

'independence' ability 118–19
'inner-directed' job orientation
35, 37, 39, 39, 40
'in-service' experience *see* work
experience
institution types 7–9, 12, 74,
93–108, 140, 143
A-level results 30, 31–2
career development 105–7,
106
degree class 104, 104, 105
educational success 98, 98–9
employment differences
100–1, 102
employment status 94–8, 95,
96, 97
job types 80, 82
mature students 43
research sample 15, 15–16
salaries 103, 103, 104
social background 99, 100–2,
104, 105
intellectual skills 111, 117,
118–19, 120–1
interactive skills *see* social skills
'intrinsic' goals 33, 34, 41

job orientation 34–9, 35–6, 39,
40
job quality 105–8, 106
job recruitment profile 75–84,
76–80, 81–3, 85–7
job types 74–5, 76–80, 80, 81, 88
educational success 83, 84
employing organisation
100–1, 102
institution attended 80, 82
social background 84, 85–6
journalism jobs *see* job types

laboratory technician jobs *see* job types
labour market 3, 26, 27, 48–56, 57–73, 142–3
  employment trends 49–51
  graduate 51–5
  segmentation 55–6
  student perceptions of 58, 98
  see also graduate destinations
law courses *see* subject areas: 1982 panel; subject areas: 1985 panel
leadership skills *118–19, 120–1*, 122, *125*, 125, *126*, 131, *132*, 135
legal services jobs *see* job types
'leisure' job orientation 36, 37–8, *39, 40*
librarianship courses *14, 17*, 35, 36
local government employers *see* employing organisations
logic skills *118–19*

male graduates *see* gender
management jobs *see* job types
manual work, fathers' 85, *86*, 99
manufacturing employers *see* employing organisations
marketing sales work *88*
married status, and career progression 89, 90, *89, 90*, 91, *91, 92*
mathematics courses *14, 17*, 35, 36
Maths O-level results *98*, 111, *113*, 113–14
mature students 6, 22, 24, 30, 48, 54
  course type 43, *45*
  job orientation *39, 40*
mechanical engineering courses *see* subject areas: 1985 panel
modern languages courses *see* subject areas: 1982 panel; subject areas: 1985 panel
music jobs *see* job types

non-management jobs *see* job types
numeracy skills 111, 117, *118–19, 120–1*, 122–3, *124*, 126–8, *127*, 131
  work experience benefit *132*, 134
nursing courses *14, 17*, 35, 36, *126*

occupation, fathers' *see* family background

Occupational Studies Group (OSG) 60
oil mining employment *87*
O-level results 42–3, *98*, 99
  English *98*, 112–13, *112*
  Maths *98*, 111, *113*, 113–14
oral communication *see* spoken communication
'organising' ability *118–19*
Oxbridge candidates 96–7

panel surveys 11, 12–21, *13–14*, *15–16, 18–19, 20*
parents *see* family background
part-time employment 49, 50, 52, *89, 90*
performing arts courses *see* subject areas: 1985 panel
permanent relationships and career progress 89, 90, *89*, *90, 91, 91, 92*
'personal interest' as study motivation *38, 39*, 143
personnel jobs *see* job types
pharmacy courses *14, 17*, 35, 36, *126*
policy, government 6–7
'political awareness' skills *118–19*
polytechnic employers *87*
polytechnics 8, 140
  1985 panel contact 15, *15*
  universities/BTEC compared *see* institution types
'pragmatic' (extrinsic) goals 33, 34
pre-labour market segmentation 55, 60–1
'presentation' skills *132*
private sector employment 142
problem-solving skills 111, 131, *132, 133*
production engineering courses *14, 17*, 35, 36, *126*
production engineering jobs *see* job types
production industries 49
production management jobs *see* job types
professional services sector 52, 53
programming jobs *see* job types
psychology courses *14, 17*, 35, 36
public relations jobs *see* job types
public sector employment *see* employing organisations

qualification types 12
  see also degree class

quantity surveying courses *see* subject areas: 1985 panel
questionnaires 11, 21

recruitment trends 59–60
research methods 11–21
  cohort comparisons 20, *20*
  course samples 12–15, *13–14*
  graduate selection 15–16, *17*, *18–19, 19–20*
response rates, graduates *17*, *18–19, 19–20*
'responsibility' ability *118–19, 126*
retail employers *see* employing organisation
retail management jobs *see* job types
retail sales jobs *see* job types

salaries *103*, 103, 104–5, *104*
  employer type *87*
  gender and family formation 88–9, 90, *90*
samples, research 15–16, *15–16*, 19–20
schools, as employers *see* employing organisations
schools, fee-paying 46, *46*, 84, 85, *86*, 99, 100–1
science courses *see* subject areas: 1982 panel; subject areas: 1985 panel
science research jobs *see* job types
secretarial jobs *see* job types
selection of graduates 15–16, *17, 18–19, 19–20*
'self-confidence' ability *118–19*, 131, *132, 133*
self-employment 49, 50, 52, *89*
service industries 49, 51–2, 52
'shortages', graduate 6, 10
single status, and career progress 89, 90, *89, 90, 91, 92*
social background 6, 22–3, 140, 141
  course types 46–7, *46*, 99, 100–2
  job orientation *39, 40*
  job types 84, *85, 86*
  salaries 104–5, *104*
'social catchment' 4, 24, 27, 40–7, 44, 45, 46, 140
social class *see* social background
social demand for higher education 33–9, *35–6, 38, 39, 40, 47*
social profile *see* social background

social science courses *see* subject areas: 1982 panel; subject areas: 1985 panel
social skills 111, 117, *118–19*, *120–1*, 125
social welfare jobs *see* job types
speed of entry into labour market *see* employment take-up
spoken communication 117, *118–19, 120–1, 122, 124, 126, 127*
sport courses *see* subject areas: 1985 panel
student aspirations *see* student orientations
student characteristics 3, 4
  see also educational experience; social background; student orientations
student evaluation 111, 143–4
  satisfaction with course 114–22, *114, 115, 116, 119*
  transferable skills 122–8, *123, 124, 125, 126, 127*
  work experience benefits 130, *132, 133, 134, 135, 136*
student orientations 2–3, 22, 23–4, *26, 27–8*, 94, 139, 141
  job orientations 34–9, *35–6, 38, 39*
'study commitment', as work experience benefit 132
subject areas 12, 52–3, 58, 60–1, 107, 139, 141–2
  1982 panel 12–13, *13–14*
    basic skills required *112, 113*
    employment status 67, 70–3
    gender differences 44
    job orientation *35, 36*
    response rates 17
    speed of labour market entry 63
    transferable skills *120–1, 126*
  1985 panel 13, *13–14*
    A-level points *31, 32, 98*
    basic skills required *112, 113*
    employment status 69, 70–3
    employment type 100
    fathers' occupation *46, 99*
    further study reasons 38
    job quality *106*
    job types 75, *76–80*
    mature students 45
    O-level passes *98*
    response rates *18–19*

salaries *103, 104*
satisfaction with course *114, 115, 116*
secondary school attended *46, 99*
social background *99, 104*
speed of labour market entry 63
transferable skills *118–19, 120–1, 123–5, 126, 127*
work experience benefits 130, *132–5, 136*
surveying jobs *see* job types
systems analysis jobs *see* job types

teaching jobs *see* job types
technical college employment 87
technological change 49, 138
textile and fashion design courses *see* subject areas: 1982 panel; subject areas: 1985 panel
'thematic' ('vocationally diffuse') subjects 62, 71–2, 95, 139
Three Dimensional Design courses *see* subject areas: 1982 panel; subject areas: 1985 panel
time comparisons 3–4, 5, 12
training 97, 105–6, *106*
transferable skills 110–11, 117–28, *118–21, 123–5, 126, 127, 136, 137,* 142
transport employers 87

'understanding other people' ability *118–19*
unemployment 6, 52, 139
  family formation *89, 90*
  gender and subject area 67, *69, 70, 71, 72*
  universities/polytechnics compared 95, *95,* 102
universities
  1985 panel contact 15, *16*
  polytechnics/BTEC compared *see* institution types
university employers 87, 88, 100
University of Warwick Institute of Employment Research 59

'vocational' subjects 62, 63, 70, 72, 141–2, 143
'vocationally diffuse' subjects *see* 'thematic' subjects

welfare jobs *see* job types
women *see* gender
work experience 128–36, *130, 132, 133, 134, 135, 136,* 137
written communication 117, *118–19, 120–1, 122, 123*

'year of graduation' effects 72

Name Index

Acker, S. 41
Ball, C. 28, 30
Boys, C. 7, 9, 55, 94, 96, 114, 115, 116, 129, 131
Bradshaw, D. 111
Brennan, J. 6, 7, 9, 11, 12, 25, 30, 55, 59, 60, 61, 114, 117
Cox, R. 52, 53, 59, 60
Craigh, S. 50
Creigh, S. 52
Curwen, P. 129
DES 59–60, 128
Dippelhofer-Stien, B. 34
Employment Gazette 51
Fleming, A. 50
Gatley, D. 43
Harvey, B. 29, 41
IMS (Institute of Manpower Studies) 41, 49
Jepson, M. 7, 94
Kirkland, J. 55, 94, 96, 114, 115, 116, 131
Lyon, E.S. 49, 110, 125
McGeevor, P. 6, 9, 11, 12, 25, 30, 55, 59, 60, 61, 114, 117
Meadows, P. 52, 53, 59, 60
Morgan, W.J. 111
Murray, K. 49
National Advisory Body 110
Pearson, R. 49, 51, 54, 110, 111
Phillips, C. 54
Pike, G. 51, 110
Piper, D. Warren 41
Rajan, A. 49
Redpath, B. 29, 41
Rees, A. 52
Roizen, J. 7, 94
Sanyal, B.C. 34
Scott, N. 59, 111
Silver, H. 7, 9, 25
Tarsh, J. 52, 54
Teichler, U. 144
Thomas, K. 41
Wilson, R.A. 53